WORLD BANK WORKING PAPER NO. 67

Microfinance in Russia

*Broadening Access to Finance for Micro
and Small Entrepreneurs*

Sylvie K. Bossoutrot

THE WORLD BANK
Washington, D.C.

332
B74m

  Cal   printed on recycled paper

ISBN-10: 0-8213-6386-7   ISBN-13: 978-0-8213-6386-7
eISBN: 0-8213-6387-5
ISSN: 1726-5878   DOI: 10.1596/978-0-8213-6386-7
Cover photo by Yuri Kozyrev, 2002.

Sylvie K. Bossoutrot is Senior Operations Officer in the Private and Financial Sectors Development unit of the Europe and Central Asia region at the World Bank.

Library of Congress Cataloging-in-Publication Data

Bossoutrot, Sylvie K., 1969-
    Microfinance in Russia : broadening access to finance for micro and small entrepreneurs / Sylvie Bossoutrot.
        p. cm.—(World Bank working paper ; no. 67)
    Includes bibliographical references.
    ISBN-13: 978-0-8213-6386-7
        1. Microfinance—Russia (Federation) 2. Financial services industry—Russia (Federation) 3. Small business—Russia (Federation)—Finance. I. Title. II. Series.

HG178.33.R8B67 2005
332—dc22

                                                            2005052338

Contents

Preface

This paper aims to provide an overview of the state of development of the microfinance industry in the Russian Federation. The paper will highlight the role played by microfinance in Russia to date, describe the main institutional types of provider as well as their outreach and performance, and present emerging industry trends. It will also discuss key challenges to the sustainable development and growth of the industry based on constraints identified in the policy, legal, and regulatory environment as well as capacity building needs of the key providers.

Recent studies have been conducted outside the World Bank on the demand for microfinance in Russia and early constraints in the legal and regulatory framework faced by microfinance institutions. The proposed study was structured so as not to duplicate previous efforts but to provide an updated overview and further the analysis on the main trends and challenges that could constrain the development of the industry.

This report was prepared by Sylvie Bossoutrot (Senior Operations Officer, ECSPF) with technical inputs and guidance from Bikki Randhawa (Senior Financial Specialist, FSE) based on the findings of a first mission conducted in April 2004 and followup field work. Important contribution on financial sector issues was made by Paula Perttunen (Lead Financial Specialist, ECSPF). Yevgeni Krasnov (Financial Analyst), Igor Zimin (Consultant), Maya Meredova (Consultant), and Dmitri Gaitudinov (Consultant) also provided valuable assistance in data collection and analysis. The note draws on existing analytical material, site visits, interviews and discussions with market participants, government officials, and donors.

The team extends special thanks to Nikolas Drude (Advisor to URCC) for his excellent contribution and support throughout the report's preparation and to Martin Holtmann (Lead Financial Specialist, CGAP), Neil Parison (Managing Director, Bannock Consulting), and Gail Buyske (Banking Consultant) for their extensive peer review. The team also expresses its gratitude to the Russian Microfinance Center, ACDI/VOCA, URCC, DID, USAID, DAI, and microfinance providers (KMB Bank, FORA, RWMN, FINCA, RCCDF, and Alternativa) that provided crucial information on their activities and generously gave their time to share their knowledge and insights of the market.

Acronyms and Abbreviations

BNB	Banco de Nordeste do Brasil
BRI	Bank Rakyat Indonesia
CAMELS	Capital adequacy, Asset quality, Management, Earnings, Liquidity, and Sensitivity
CARD	Center for Agriculture and Rural Development
CBR	Bank of Russia
CEF	Counterpart Enterprise Fund
CFIs	Cooperative financial institution
CGAP	Consultative Group to Assist the Poorest
CIDA	Canadian International Development Agency
CIS	Commonwealth of Independent States
DAI	Development Alternatives Inc.
DFID	U.K. Department for International Development
DID	Développement International Desjardins
DRC	Danish Refugee Council
EBRD	European Bank for Reconstruction and Development
EU	European Union
FIDP	Financial Institutions Development Project (World Bank)
FOREX	Foreign exchange
GDP	Gross domestic product
IDB	Inter-American Development Bank
IFC	International Finance Corporation
KfW	Kreditanstalt für Wiederaufbau (German development bank)
KMB	Bank Kreditovanye Malovo Bisnesa foreign-owned microfinance bank in Russia
KSBP	Kazakhstan Small Business Program
MEB	Micro-enterprise bank
MFI	Microfinance institution
MIX	Microfinance Information eXchange
MOEDT	Ministry of Economic Development and Trade
MOF	Ministry of Finance
NACSCU	National Association of Cooperative Savings and Credit Unions
OECD	Organisation for Economic Co-operation and Development
PEARLS	Protection, Effective financial structure, Asset quality, Rates of return and costs, Liquidity, and Signs of growth
RCC	Rural Credit Cooperative
RCCDF	Rural Credit Cooperatives Development Fund
RDB	Russian Development Bank
RMC	Russian Microfinance Center
RROA	Return on average assets
RROE	Return on average equity
RSBF	Russia Small Business Fund

RWMN	Russian Women's Microfinance Network
SME	Small and medium-size enterprise
SSEDF	Sakhalin Small Enterprise Development Foundation
TACIS	Technical Assistance for the CIS
TAISP	Targeted Awards-Innovation Support Program
TUSRIF	U.S. Russian Investment Fund
UNDP	United Nations Development Programme
URCC	Union of Rural Credit Cooperative
USAID	United States Agency for International Development
USDA	U.S. Department of Agriculture
VAT	Value-added tax
VTB	Vneshtorgbank
WOCCU	World Council of Credit Unions

Executive Summary

Microfinance has emerged over the past 30 years as a mechanism to deliver small-scale financial services on a commercial basis to the financially underserved—a category that includes low-income households and micro-entrepreneurs who are typically considered "nonbankable" by the mainstream financial sector.

The microfinance approach to development is predicated on the assumption that low-income households and micro-entrepreneurs, as all economic agents, need and can benefit from a wide range of financial products including credit, savings, money transfer, and insurance services. These services can empower them to take advantage of business opportunities, increase their earning potential, manage risk, and build assets.

By providing financial services to the underserved, microfinance has thus emerged as a vehicle to fight poverty by stimulating economic development and social inclusion. At the same time, it has been noted that microfinance should not be misconstrued for a welfare or social assistance tool. Poverty alleviation also depends on the poor having access to food, shelter, basic social services, a stable political environment, and market opportunities. Microfinance is thus *not* the appropriate instrument for all segments of the poor. It is generally most appropriate where some forms of economic activity already exist as it may otherwise create an excessive debt burden for the destitute (CGAP 2002).

Over the past three decades, microfinance has evolved from being a *movement* driven primarily by social returns to becoming an *industry* guided increasingly by standards and commercial bottom line. The success and exponential increase of microfinance supply around the world has been based largely on two important realizations: (1) that the poor can be reliable borrowers and pay high interest rates, and (2) that microfinance providers can thus cover their costs and even become profitable.

Today there is an estimated 68 million microfinance borrowers worldwide, which represents an almost fivefold increase over the past six years. Loans outstanding are estimated to amount to some $15 billion. Loan sizes vary greatly by region and by country but in general tend to range from a few dollars up to several thousand dollars. Approximately one-third of these loans are made by commercial banks, one-third by cooperative banks and credit unions, and one-third by specialized microfinance institutions.

Notwithstanding the global growth of microfinance, demand for microfinance services continues to vastly outstrip the current level of supply. The Consultative Group to Assist the Poorest (CGAP) calculated that, in 2004, microfinance institutions covered only one-third of their target market's estimated demand for savings and loan products.[1]

For many microfinance providers that—with the exception of large-scale institutions such as Bank Rakyat Indonesia (BRI) and Grameen Bank in Bangladesh—remain small, one of the foremost challenges is thus to scale up while controlling their costs.

---

1. CGAP is a consortium established by 28 public and private development agencies to promote sustainable microfinance through common and harmonized standards and norms. It is housed in the World Bank.

In this respect, a number of noteworthy industry developments have taken place over the past several years which have allowed retail providers to both expand and reach higher levels of sustainability:

■ *Microfinance institutions (MFIs) are increasingly using standard performance measurements and exploring new sources of funding.* The use of standard performance calculations has been encouraged by industry benchmarking associations such as the Microfinance Information eXchange (MIX), to which close to 400 microfinance providers report semiannually.[2] The emergence of specialized microfinance rating agencies has also encouraged MFIs to improve their financial reporting. Standardized reporting and enhanced transparency have, in turn, increased MFIs' ability to attract private sector investors such as equity funds. Several microfinance organizations have also issued debt in their local capital markets. A noteworthy example is that of the Mexican MFI, Financiera Compartamos, which was the first MFI to issue unsecured debt in 2002.

■ *Some MFIs have transformed into formal institutions.* This trend was initiated by BancoSol in Bolivia, which started as a nongovernmental organization (NGO) named Prodem in the 1980s and became a full-fledged bank in 1992. There has since been various examples of microfinance institutions that have undertaken transformation to support their growth strategy. This includes CARD (Center for Agriculture and Rural Development) in the Philippines, which transformed into a rural bank in 1997. CARD had less than 500 clients in the early 1990s; it has over 55,000 today.

■ *MFIs are moving from only credit to a wider range of financial products and exploring new delivery channels.* The quest for sustainability and increased understanding of the needs of micro-entrepreneurs is leading MFIs to introduce a wider range of products in order to grow and maximize their return on operations. Some of these products include insurance, mortgage finance, leasing, savings products, credit cards, and remittances. MFIs are also exploring ways to increase their delivery capacity by cooperating with organizations that have large distribution networks, such as post offices and bank networks.

In Russia, microfinance has emerged as a mechanism to support self-employment and small-scale entrepreneurship primarily in trade and services, which developed in response to the transition and collapse of large state-owned enterprises of the early 1990s.

While microfinance in the developing world emerged to address the needs of largely uneducated and semiskilled workforces, in Russia as in neighboring transition countries, it emerged as a vehicle to support a well-educated class of "new poor" who turned to self-employment out of necessity.

---

2.   MIX is a nonprofit benchmarking association supported by CGAP, the Citigroup Foundation, the Open Society Institute, the Rockdale Foundation, and other foundations. It collects financial and portfolio data provided voluntarily by leading microfinance institutions and organizes the data by peer groups. The primary purpose of this database is to help MFI managers and board members understand their performance in comparison to other MFIs. Secondary objectives include establishing industry performance standards, enhancing the transparency of financial reporting, and improving the performance of microfinance institutions.

Despite policymakers' recurrent reference to the importance of small business as an engine of growth and market foundation, the enterprise sector in Russia has enjoyed little effective government support and continues, to a large extent, to be dominated by large, vertically integrated financial industrial groups.

In the absence of a more conducive environment where middle to large diversified enterprises can emerge and contribute to growth and employment, small-scale entrepreneurship and self-employment have thus played a critical role in preventing low-income and unemployed individuals from falling into poverty.

Russia's banking sector ability to reach small-scale entrepreneurs has been marginal. Although bank assets have more than tripled in the past five years, the banking sector remains small in comparison to developed or even transition economies. Financial intermediation thus remains low, with rural areas being particularly underserved. Over 80 percent of all bank assets are concentrated in Moscow or the Moscow region while the large state-controlled savings bank, Sberbank, which accounts for 70 percent of retail deposits, continues to withdraw from loss-making rural areas and small towns.

In addition, few Russian banks are organizationally geared toward micro and small enterprise lending. This may reflect the initial investment required in setting up retail branch networks to reach small clients, the inability of banks to pass cost-effective adequate judgment on the quality of credits (leading to the perpetuation of an asset-based lending culture), the high regulatory cost related to small loans, and the banks' difficulties to secure acceptable and liquid collateral. SME lending thus continues to a large extent to be perceived by banks as a high-risk and high-cost activity.

To fund their businesses, micro-entrepreneurs thus tend to rely primarily on their own funds or borrow from family and friends. Lack of access to formal external sources of finance has also led to the development of a burgeoning industry of money lenders and loan sharks lending at 10 percent or more per month.

It is in this context of severe shortage of access to finance that microfinance institutions of different types have emerged to meet the unfulfilled financing needs of micro-entrepreneurs.

There are typically four institutional types of providers in the global microfinance delivery system: (1) commercial banks (downscaling and greenfield), (2) specialized NGO-type MFIs, (3) membership-based institutions such as rural cooperatives and credit unions, and (4) public funds.

While all four types of institutions have emerged in Russia, the industry remains in the early stages of development and is yet to reach scale: KMB Bank, Russia's foreign-owned microfinance bank, has about 34,000 loans outstanding; FORA Fund (by far the largest NGO MFI) has about 16,000 active clients. Credit cooperatives unite some 420,800 members. Data on regional funds are sketchy. Absence of centralized standardized information on the scope of their activities prevents an assessment of the depth of their outreach. However, official data obtained on 21 regional and municipal funds involved in microfinance programs suggests that, in aggregate terms, their client base does not exceed 10,000 borrowers.

Despite a slow start, owing largely to the unclear legal environment of the early 1990s, the microfinance industry has been growing at an accelerated pace over the past three to five years. A more detailed analysis of the sector reveals a number of emerging industry trends:

■ *Russian microfinance providers use the two traditional methodological models used by providers across the world:* (1) the Group lending model originated by Grameen

Bank whereby all group members are responsible for the timely repayment of any loan to any single member of the group, and (2) individual lending. Loan sizes vary but, on average, tend to be higher than those in Latin America or Asia and range from a few hundred dollars to $10,000 or more depending on providers and regions. Loan repayment rates are high and portfolio quality of MFIs in the East Europe and Central Asia region (ECA) is higher on average than that of any other region.

▓ *The microfinance industry has been largely developed as a result of donor initiatives and technical assistance support.* As in other ECA countries, many of Russia's microfinance providers have relied on donor assistance for their development.

▓ *EBRD has played a prominent role in promoting bank microlending* through its Russia Small Business Fund (RSBF) program and, in 1999, established KMB bank—Russia's foreign-owned greenfield microfinance bank.

▓ *EBRD's microfinance program tend to serve the high end of the micro and small enterprise market* and provides larger loans to larger businesses than other MFIs do. RSBF borrowers also tend to be established, urban-based entrepreneurs who have been in business for three years or more.

▓ *While the greenfield microfinance model has been quite successful, the jury is still out on the downscaling model.* Although KMB Bank's performance has provided evidence that microfinance banking can work in Russia with the introduction of appropriate lending technology, the donor-driven and subsidy-intensive downscaling model has not delivered the expected scale and outreach.

▓ *While commercial banks are not dominant players in microfinance, there has been significant growth in consumer lending over the past couple of years*—a portion of which may have been used for small business finance purposes. While the observed surge in consumer lending reflects a true increase in *pure* retail lending such as household goods, car or mortgage loans, it also reflects an increase in small business lending as many Russian individual entrepreneurs use consumer credits to finance their business needs.

▓ *The credit cooperative sector is expanding rapidly.* There has been a dramatic growth in the number and membership base of urban and agricultural credit cooperatives in the past five years, notably in southern Russia. This rapid growth occurred despite the fragmented legal and regulatory framework governing cooperatives and their limited access to funding.

▓ *Cooperatives and in particular rural cooperatives have emerged as a complement to the banking sector.* The ongoing retreat of banks from already underbanked rural areas and small communities has deprived increasing numbers of family farms and rural-based entrepreneurs of access to finance. Credit cooperatives have emerged to fill this gap.

▓ *The cooperative sector is unsupervised.* As the membership and asset size of most credit cooperatives have tended thus far to remain small, Russian authorities have only recently started to look into the issue of regulation and supervision of the cooperative sector.

▓ *Scale and outreach of NGO operations remain limited.* While pilot operations have been established in Siberia and the Far East, the majority remains concentrated in the Western part of the country. Most operations remain small and tend to be concentrated in urban areas of 200,000 inhabitants or more.

■ *NGO MFI clients are mainly micro-entrepreneurs engaged in retail trade.* The over-whelming majority of clients are low-income micro-entrepreneurs concentrated in the retail trade sector and services with a large number of women. Manufacturing businesses represent a marginal fraction of their clientele. Average loan size tend to be below $2,000, suggesting that NGO MFIs reach a lower end of the market than does KMB Bank. Maturities and interest rates vary by region and organization but tend to range from 24 to 72 percent per annum.

■ *NGOs are looking to transform as a postdonor support strategy.* Absence of a clear legal and regulatory framework for NGO MFIs and decreasing donor funding have led some leading NGO providers to explore transformation options. The Russian Women's Microfinance Network (RWMN) is seeking to transform into a nonbank credit organization while FORA is in the process of transforming into a full-fledged bank and FINCA is planning to become a commercial company. Lead-ing providers have also started to look for commercial sources of funding and are trying to develop partnerships with foreign and domestic banks.

■ *Microfinance providers of all types are expanding their product range.* Key providers are seeking to scale up their operations and keep up with the competition by broadening their product line. For example, credit unions, faced with increased competition from banks in the area of consumer lending, are looking to expand their small business lending portfolio and develop new products such as mort-gage loans.

Despite the recent growth, a study conducted by the Russian Microfinance Center and SME Resource Center estimated that the volume of supply of microcredits covers less than 5 per-cent of the potential market—suggesting that microfinance has a considerable unrealized upside potential.

To live up to expectations and deliver financial services to a larger number of under-served individuals including in remote areas, microfinance providers will thus need to scale up significantly. This will require the collaborative efforts of both policymakers and industry providers.

Policymakers in Russia need to recognize MFIs' potential in stimulating entrepreneur-ship and providing financial services to the underserved and need to integrate microfinance into the mainstream financial sector by creating a clear enabling legal and regulatory envi-ronment. Given the recent accelerated growth observed in the cooperatives sector, devel-oping an adequate regulatory and supervisory framework for both credit unions and rural credit cooperatives will be a critical undertaking. In designing this framework, policymak-ers will need to consider and weigh a number of issues including: (1) how to introduce pru-dential and nonprudential guidelines that would ensure the sound development of the sector and protect the growing number of member depositors without suffocating the industry, and (2) which model of supervision to adopt taking into consideration the cur-rent capacity and burden imposed on supervisory authorities and assessing the potential for industry self-regulation.

Russian microfinance providers, as in the rest of the world, are faced with a double challenge—the challenge of self-sufficiency (that is, graduating away from donor dependence and subsidy) and the challenge of keeping a strong poverty outreach (that is, reaching the financially underserved and the poor). To meet these challenges, as donors scale back, Russian MFIs will need to develop new products and explore new delivery channels and sources of funding to support their continued growth. They will need to make themselves more attractive to commercial funders by improving their performance and increasing the transparency of their financial reporting. To reach scale and streamline their delivery cost, MFIs may also need to explore different partnership options with commercial banks and/or among themselves. Finally, as some NGO MFIs have started to do, mature providers may wish to explore different transformation options including transformation into more formal financial institutions.

CHAPTER 1

Background

Global Experience in Microfinance

Poverty is aggravated by disadvantaged groups' restricted access to finance. Research shows that access to financial services can be an important tool for preventing people from falling into—or moving out of—poverty. As all economic agents, low-income households and micro-entrepreneurs can benefit from credit, savings, and insurance services. These services can help them take advantage of business opportunities, increase their earning potential, build assets, and reduce vulnerability to external shocks. Without access to finance from professional service providers, low-income and disadvantaged groups have to rely on informal sources of funding such as family, friends, or money lenders and may become targets of predatory schemes. Financial exclusion and restricted access to financial services thus reduces the potential welfare of individuals and the productivity of enterprises in an economy.[3]

Formal financial markets typically fail to serve the poor. Because low-income individuals tend to have insufficient traditional forms of collateral, they are often excluded from financial services offered by banks. High transaction costs relative to the small size of loans typically required by the poor also make microfinance unattractive to mainstream formal financial institutions, particularly in remote areas with low population density. As a rule,

---

3. World Bank (2004a). The importance of wider access to finance for more equitable growth was also underscored by Rajan and Zingales in a widely noted publication, *Saving Capitalism from the Capitalists:* "Many of the evils of capitalism—the tyranny of capital over labor, the excessive concentration of industry, the unequal distribution of income in favor of the owners of capital, the relative lack of opportunity for the poor—can be attributed, in some if not substantial measure, to the underdevelopment of finance. . . . Given the right infrastructure, however, financiers can overcome the tyranny of collateral and connections and make credit available even to the poor. They become a power for the good rather than the guardians of the status quo."

traditional formal financial service providers, such as banks, thus often fail to serve low-income households and micro-enterprises (World Bank 2001).

Microfinance has emerged as an alternative vehicle for serving the segments of the population considered "nonbankable" by formal banking institutions. Its role as an effective tool to serve the poor and provide financing to micro-entrepreneurs and thus help create jobs has gained increasing global recognition. The important role played by microfinance in broadening access to finance for the underserved was highlighted by the G-8 in June 2004[4] and the United Nations Social and Economic Council proclaimed 2005 the International Year of Microcredit.

While microfinance originally emerged in the late 1970s as a tool to alleviate poverty in developing countries, Western economies have started to emulate the successful experiences of the developing world. The small enterprise sector constitutes a significant part of developed countries' economies and is an important source of employment. In Western Europe alone, two million enterprises are created every year, 90 percent of which have fewer than five employees.[5] Because in Western economies access to external finance for the self-employed and for small start-up enterprises also remains limited, microfinance schemes have started to emerge as a mechanism to bridge this financing gap in complement to the mainstream banking sector. In 2003, a European Microfinance Network was established to support the development of microfinance in Western Europe and promote self-employment in response to growing unemployment levels. By end-2004, the network included 28 organizations from 15 European Union (EU) member states.[6]

Microfinance is best suited to serve the working poor. Poverty alleviation also depends on the poor having access to food, shelter, basic social services (such as education and health), a stable political environment, and market opportunities. Microfinance should thus not be misconstrued for a welfare or social assistance tool and cannot replace social programs targeted at deep pockets of poverty. It is generally most appropriate where some forms of economic activity already exist as it may otherwise create an excessive debt burden for the destitute (CGAP 2002).

Microfinance has evolved significantly since the early days of microcredit. As the poor need a variety of financial services, microfinance has evolved from pure credit to a broader range of financial services such as savings, remittances, leasing, housing, and insurance products. The vision for the microfinance industry accordingly has shifted from the provision of only credit to a more permanent access to financial services through a broad range of financial institutional types. Examples from global experience show that microfinance providers vary from informal channels (membership-based savings and credit associations) and semiformal (NGOs) to formal institutions (banks).

Demand for microfinance vastly outstrips the supply. Although supply and demand data are mostly country specific, CGAP calculated that, in 2004, microfinance institutions

---

4. G-8 Summit in Sea Island, Georgia (United States), June 2004.

5. In the European Union, micro-enterprises (defined as enterprises employing fewer than 10 people) represent 89 percent of all enterprises by number, 28 percent of GDP, and 21 percent of employment (Nowak 2005).

6. The French Association ADIE (Association pour le Droit a l'Initiative Economique) has been particularly successful in helping unemployed individuals start up their own businesses. Established in 1988, ADIE has funded 23,000 micro-enterprises since 1989. Loan size does not exceed 10,000 euros. Recovery rate is 94 percent (Nowak 2005).

targeting poor and near-poor clients covered only 33 percent of their target market's estimated demand for savings and loan products (CGAP 2004). Although the market for financial services required by the poor is considerable, scale remains limited with the exception of a few countries such as Bangladesh and Indonesia.

One of the foremost challenges for microfinance institutions is scaling up operations. Reaching a large number of clients while maintaining a growth path that does not compromise on institutional financial viability remains a challenge for most microfinance providers. The vast majority of MFIs operating today are not financially sustainable and continue to depend on external assistance. The MicroBanking Bulletin's data for July 2003 revealed that of 124 institutions reporting financial data, only 66 were fully self-sufficient (that is, had achieved profitability after adjusting for subsidies). In examining the global experience and looking at how some institutions have emerged and succeeded to scale up in a sustainable manner, lessons can be drawn from a number of triggers at the policy, infrastructure, and retail levels that have played an instrumental role in broadening access to finance for the underserved:

- *New specialized institutions and delivery channels have developed or reemerged to serve the micro and small market niche.* As of the end of 2004, the Europe and Central Asia region had a total of 10 new licensed, regulated, and supervised microenterprise banks (MEBs) with an estimated $984 million in over 202,000 outstanding loans and $962 million in deposits. In addition, since 1992, Poland has seen the redevelopment of a strong credit union movement uniting over 1 million members and offering a wide range of products including term deposits, long-term credits, housing loans, automated teller machine (ATM) and electronic payments services. Outside the region, a textbook example is that of BRI in Indonesia, where a new autonomous microbanking division of a large state-owned commercial bank was developed in the 1980s. By end-2004, BRI's microfinance arm, known as the Unit Desa system, had built an extensive network of over 4,000 Unit bank offices and nearly 200 service posts nationwide, with over 80 of the networks concentrated in rural areas and small towns. By August 2004, the BRI Unit Desa system had 3.1 million outstanding borrowers with a total loan portfolio of about $1.9 billion and $2.9 billion worth of deposits in 30 million savings accounts.
- *Building existing institutions' capacity has also been key to reach down market in a sustainable manner.* The European Bank for Reconstruction and Development's (EBRD) Small Business Funds in the Commonwealth of Independent States (CIS) region use a capacity-building strategy in their downscaling model and provide technical assistance to existing partner banks to develop the methodology required to reach the micro and small client base. As such, the EBRD approach is a replica of the "multiglobal loans" that the Inter-American Development Bank (IDB) extended to commercial banks in Latin America during the early 1990s. The World Council of Credit Unions (WOCCU) has also helped credit cooperatives around the world build up their membership base through capacity-building technical assistance.
- *Product development has been an important factor in scaling up operations.* Because the demand for a broad range of financial services is high, innovation in product development can be instrumental in increasing outreach and retaining clients. The

experience of BRI Unit Desa in launching savings products that meet the clients' needs was instrumental to the success of its branch network. Some of BRI's savings products have stood the test of time and continue to be in high demand years after the products' development and launch. An increasing number of microfinance organizations have also been testing other new generations of products such as micro-insurance, microleasing, housing microfinance, and remittances.

▨ *Use of standard performance measurements has allowed MFIs to broaden their access to private sources of funding.* Use of standard performance calculations has been encouraged by industry benchmarking associations such as MIX, to which close to 400 providers report semiannually.[7] The emergence of specialized rating agencies has also encouraged MFIs to improve their financial reporting. In 2003, a record number of over 100 MFIs were rated. This increased their ability to access private sector investors such as equity funds. Several microfinance organizations have also issued debt in their local capital markets. A noteworthy example was that of the Mexican MFI, Financiera Compartamos, which was the first to issue unsecured debt in July 2002 through a peso bond of about $15 million equivalent (Buyske 2005).

▨ *Financial infrastructure and technology can help increase the volume and velocity of financial services.* Microfinance operations can benefit from credit information bureaus, credit scoring techniques, automated central registry systems, electronic banking, and smart cards. Automated central registry systems for rights to real property and moveable collateral can reduce the transaction and processing costs to microfinance institutions when security in the form of collateral is involved in the loan procedure. The World Bank has for example assisted the Government of Romania in the latter's efforts to address the structural causes of the problems related to limited availability of collateral, notably for rural credit, by helping design a modern legal and regulatory framework for secured transactions with movable assets and develop an automated central registry system.

▨ *Flexible legal and regulatory frameworks capable of adapting to the market play a key role in addressing access to finance.* MFIs change and develop as the scale and scope of their operations grow beyond the delivery of credit services to include savings, deposits, and other financial services. To increase their autonomy and access new financial sources capable of supporting their growth strategy, a number of MFIs set out to obtain licenses as banks or nonbank financial institutions. This trend was initiated by BancoSol in Bolivia, which started as an NGO named Prodem in the 1980s and became a full-fledged bank in 1992 when the Bolivian Superintendency of Banks and Financial Entities approved the creation of BancoSol as a commercial bank.[8] There have since been various examples of MFIs that through transformation from a semiformal institution to a formal intermediary have vastly increased their outreach and become sustainable. In the Philippines, for example, the Center for Agriculture and Rural Development (CARD) was established as an

---

7. MIX's mission is to help build the microfinance market infrastructure by offering data sourcing, benchmarking and performance monitoring tools, and specialized microfinance information services. See note 2 for details.

8. In 2002, BancoSol was the largest bank in Bolivia in terms of number of clients, with 35 percent of all borrowers. In 2003, it had a loan portfolio of approximately $91 million (Buyske 2005).

NGO in 1986. CARD had less than 500 clients in the early 1990s and has now over 55,000 clients in various provinces. The key to CARD's growth was its transformation in 1997 into a rural bank.

■ *The role of government in fostering a conducive policy environment for microfinance is key to the sustainable growth of the industry.* The role of government is critical in supporting policy areas that impact the sustainable development of microfinance. Key policy issues include supporting interest rate liberalization, ensuring that government-run programs do not distort the market and crowd out private sector providers, and adjusting legal and regulatory frameworks to support the development of a wide range of financial service providers and ensure the soundness of financial institutions that collect savings from the public.

Microfinance in Russia—Setting the Stage

Poverty reduction is a key priority of President Vladimir Putin's economic policy. The importance of poverty reduction was underscored by President Putin in his May 2004 Address to the Federal Assembly of the Russian Federation, in which he highlighted the government's four major long-term objectives: "doubling the gross domestic product, *reducing the number of poor people, improving the living standards of the population,* and modernizing the armed forces." Since the 1998 financial crisis, Russia has succeeded in cutting poverty in half. More favorable economic conditions increased the demand for labor and led to significant wage increases and reduction in unemployment. In addition to higher earnings, households benefited from the improved fiscal position of the government. Higher oil revenues enabled the government to substantially reduce arrears in wages and social benefits and raise pensions and public sector wages. However, close to a fifth of the population continues to live in poverty and given that the drivers of the recent growth may no longer provide the same impetus over the medium term, President Putin's objective to further halve the incidence of poverty by 2007 will require sustained and well-targeted poverty reduction programs (World Bank 2004c).

One of the key structural obstacles to growth in Russia is the lack of economic diversification. The enterprise sector comprises mostly large, vertically integrated financial industrial groups specialized in extractive industries, on the one end of the spectrum, and micro and small enterprises engaged predominantly in trade and services, on the other end. Mid-size companies, notably in productive activities, are emerging only slowly. Russian economic growth and fiscal stability thus remain heavily dependent on natural resource exports and vulnerable to commodity price fluctuations. The oil and gas sector, which, according to World Bank estimates, accounts for an even higher percentage of the gross domestic product (GDP) than stated in official estimates (close to 25 percent instead of 9 percent) employs less than 1 percent of the workforce (World Bank 2004d).

Income distribution in Russia is also highly asymmetrical. As indicated above, overall poverty levels remain high, with an estimated 22 percent of the population living on less than $2 a day. The nature and structure of poverty in Russia are characteristic of the region as a whole. As in other transition economies, households with income below subsistence level comprise not only those fully dependent on social welfare but also working age individuals with higher education who have fallen outside economic activity during the transition.

Russia is also characterized by acute income disparities between large population centers concentrated in the Western part of the country and the rest of the territory. In 2002, regional nominal output varied by a factor of 67 between the richest and the poorest region.[9] Regional economic disparities have resulted in population migration from distant rural areas and mono-industry towns to larger, more economically dynamic population centers.

The Government of Russia has given high priority to development of the SME sector because new firm growth is expected to promote economic diversification, increase employment, and ease regional disparities. However, while SMEs account for over 95 percent of enterprises and generate over half of private sector employment in most OECD countries, Russia's performance in this area has remained modest in comparison. SMEs in Russia account for less than 15 percent of employment and have grown very slowly since the mid 1990s. Over 80 percent of Russia's SME sector is composed of micro-entrepreneurs (registered as individual entrepreneurs) with less than 10 employees.[10] Although SME development is a recurrent theme of the government's official economic policy, little actual government support has been given to the sector, which also remains hampered by high administrative barriers and limited access to finance.

The Russian banking sector remains small, fragmented, and concentrated in Western Russia. Although bank assets more than tripled in the past five years, the banking sector remains small in relation to developed or even transition economies. As of end-2004, total assets of Russian banks amounted to about $255 billion, that is, the equivalent of a medium- to large-size European commercial bank. Over half of the approximately 1,300 domestic banks are concentrated in the city of Moscow and the Moscow region. The state-controlled Sberbank still accounts for a quarter of total banking assets, some 40 percent of total deposits, and 70 percent of retail deposits. The primary function for many institutions holding banking licenses in Russia is also still limited to performing treasury functions for a group of loosely related enterprises. Thus, with one dominant state-owned bank, a handful of medium- to large-size banks, and a plethora of small "pocket banks," the structure of the banking sector is unbalanced and ill-suited to serve the needs of the economy. Financial intermediation remains low, with only 4.8 percent of fixed investments financed by bank credits in 2003, most of which go to large corporates,[11] and the small and micro-enterprise sector remains largely underserved.

The banking system is also undergoing a fundamental change. The negative impact of the 1998 financial crisis on confidence in banks is gradually receding. At the same time, the Russian banking sector is entering a major restructuring process prompted by increased competition and the introduction of the new Deposit Insurance Scheme. These pressures are expected to not only lead to a substantial reduction in the number of banks but also to a concentration of bank branch networks in large population centers and other densely populated areas. Diminishing margins and the increasing cost base will likely also force closure of branches in scarcely populated areas and areas with few "bankable" clients.

---

9. A study conducted by UNDP in 2001 based on an indicator combining several dimensions of living standards (Human Development Index) showed that if the Russian regions were treated as countries, at one end of the spectrum, Moscow would be at par with Portugal and Argentina while, at the other end, Tuva would compare to Indonesia and Nicaragua (World Bank 2004c).

10. SME Observatory, SME Resource Center, 2004.

11. Bank of Russia statistics, 2003.

There is a need and a role for a wide range of financial institutions to provide complementary products and services to those offered by the banking system. Such institutions play an important role in widening the access to finance, introducing and developing specialized products for certain segments of the economy while also putting competitive pressure on the banks. These may include mortgage banks, leasing companies, finance companies, life-insurance companies as well as different types of nonbank microfinance providers. The key challenge for the Russian financial system is how to balance the needs for access to financial services by population and economic actors nationwide while ensuring development of sustainable, economically sound, and competitive financial institutions.

The Russian authorities have not yet integrated microfinance development into their broad economic development strategy. Despite its potential contribution to entrepreneurship development, public support to microfinance has been scarce. The legal and regulatory framework for microfinance remains fragmented and is still under development. Microfinance was also only recently acknowledged in Russia's new banking sector development strategy. As will be discussed below, the Government of Russia could play a more proactive role in promoting and facilitating the development of the sector. In doing so, it would benefit from reviewing the successful recent experiences of a number of countries such as Brazil where strong government policy support coupled with targeted capacity building assistance significantly increased excluded groups' access to finance over a relatively short period of time.

CHAPTER 2

State of the Industry

The Demand Side

There is no universal definition of microfinance. It varies by country and can take different forms depending on a particular economy's level and structure of development. Broad regional variations can be observed in loan sizes, types of services, target clientele, outreach, and delivery methodologies. However, in general terms, microfinance caters to the poor and underserved segments of the population by providing "small-scale financial services . . . to people who farm or herd; operate small or microenterprises where goods are produced, recycled, repaired, or traded; provide services; work for wages or commissions; gain income from renting out small amounts of land, vehicles, draft animals, or machinery and tools, and to other individuals and local groups in developing economies, in both rural and urban areas" (World Bank and Open Society Institute 2003).

The poor in Russia have similar characteristics as the poor of other regions of the world in that they earn insufficient or irregular income, have low subsistence levels, shortage of assets, and restricted access to services and finance. At the same time, poverty in Russia, as in most neighboring transition economies, presents a number of distinctive features inherited from its socialist past and the particular circumstances of the transition.

■ *Poverty emerged as a sudden and massive phenomenon in the wake of the transition.* The transition ended the previous model based on state-run production targets and subsidies and imposed market-based relations between economic agents. Hard budget constraints resulted in barterization of the economy. Declining production and liquidity problems caused many enterprises to delay or stop paying salaries. Unemployment levels soared. At the same time, price liberalization resulted in high inflation and living standards plummeted. Economic hardships coupled with the disintegration of the social safety net and guaranteed employment of the Soviet era resulted in the emergence of a large number of "new poor." In the Europe and Central Asia region as a whole, absolute poverty rates increased from 2 to 21 percent of the population between 1988 and 1998 (Foster, Greene, and Pytkowska 2003). In Russia alone, the level of poverty escalated to 41.5 percent in 1999 (World Bank 2004c). While poverty levels have since come down substantially, according to official Goskomstat statistics, over one-fifth of the population—or 31.8 million people—still lived below the poverty line in 2003.

■ *Poverty is particularly deep and widespread in agricultural areas and mono-industry communities.* Socioeconomic development varies widely among Russia's regions. The country enjoys high levels or urbanization with two-thirds of the population living in urban areas. Thus, by number, the majority of poor households can be found in urban areas. However, poverty is deeper and more widespread in rural areas and mono-industry communities. Most collective farms saw their volume of production drop significantly (by 50 percent between 1992 and 1998). In 2001, the number of rural unemployed had reached 2 million—a third in the youngest age group of 20–29 years. Today the level of rural poverty remains significantly above the level of poverty in urban areas. Rural populations are twice as likely to be poor, with over 30 percent estimated to live in poverty compared to 15 in urban areas. There is also a high incidence of poverty in areas dependent on a single industry. Under Soviet command, economic development policies based on principles of geographical industry specialization resulted in the development of a large number of mono-industry communities throughout the country. The unraveling of heavily subsidized plants in certain areas such as coal mining settlements in Northern Russia and Siberia threw entire communities into poverty. In addition to plummeting incomes, social infrastructure services previously provided by state companies were transferred to poorly funded municipalities and sharply deteriorated.

■ *Deep pockets of poverty have also emerged in Southern Russia as a result of war.* Russia has been grappling with ethnic conflicts in the North Caucasus (Southern Okrug), where war has plunged local populations in deep levels of poverty and insecurity and stalled prospects of development.

■ *Many of Russia's new poor are highly educated.* Under socialism, heavy emphasis had been placed on education and adult literacy. Adult literacy was generally universal and the participation and completion rates of both genders were high at all levels of education. Thus, the poor in the region unlike those of developing countries are literate and many are well educated (Foster, Greene, and Pytkowska 2003). In the informal economy, it is common to encounter scientists, engineers, professors (driving unofficial street cabs or trading) who have been declared redundant in their former place of work or are seeking to supplement their low earnings.

Small-scale entrepreneurship has emerged as a response to poverty. In Russia, as in neighboring transition economies, the collapse of state ownership prompted a dramatic rise in small businesses and self-employment, which replaced state-owned enterprises as important sources of employment and income. A new category of low-income economic agents—micro-entrepreneurs—emerged in the wake of the collapse of the previous system. This new category includes both (1) "spontaneous" or vocational entrepreneurs and (2) "forced entrepreneurs" or entrepreneurs by default. Spontaneous entrepreneurs are individuals with entrepreneurial skills who have voluntarily turned to business. Given appropriate resources, business environment, and access to markets, many individuals in this group representing Russia's new entrepreneurial class would likely seek to expand their businesses and grow into larger concerns. Forced entrepreneurs, on the other hand, are individuals who have turned to self-employment out of necessity and who, provided the opportunity, would likely give up their self-employed status in exchange for a permanent job with a stable employer. This latter category also includes low-income working individuals who turned to self-employment as a means to supplement their income.

Despite the broad recognition of the role of the private sector as a vital engine of economic growth, job creation, and poverty reduction, the enterprise sector in Russia has enjoyed little support and has been constrained by a number of factors ranging from excessive government regulation (which encouraged rent-seeking behavior and corruption), lack of access to finance, and underdeveloped supply chain relationships between large and small businesses. Together, these factors have contributed to shape the enterprise sector of the post-Soviet era into an unbalanced sector with large, vertically integrated, financial industrial groups concentrated in extractive industries on the one hand, and small and micro-entrepreneurs primarily engaged in trade and service activities on the other (see Box 1.)

In the absence of a more conducive environment where medium-size to large diversified enterprises can emerge and contribute to growth and employment, small-scale enterprises and self-employment have thus played a critical role in preventing low-income and/or unemployed individuals from falling into poverty.

Microfinance has emerged as a mechanism to support small-scale entrepreneurship in complement to the banking sector. In most cases, small businesses that require modest amounts of external finance (under $10,000) lack adequate collateral and credit history and are considered "nonbankable" by the mainstream financial sector. Lack of information about the business also constitutes a major deterrent for banks to lend. Small companies are usually self-financed and use funds generated internally from business operations and/or borrowed from friends, family, and partners. Anticipating rejection, small businesses may even refrain from applying for bank credits. Low-income individuals unable to get financing from mainstream banks have and would likely turn to microfinance providers for first financial external aid for business development. Microcredits are thus often the first step in the continuum of credit necessary to support the maturation of companies.

In Russia, as in neighboring transition countries, MFIs have emerged largely to meet the unfulfilled financing needs of micro-entrepreneurs. The development of the industry has thus been primarily driven by an enterprise development agenda.

The need for microfinance may be greater in lower-income regions. As noted above, there are significant differences in living standards between regions in Russia. The Russian SME Resource Center conducted an analysis of the relationship between the social and economic level of development of a given region and the share of sole proprietors in the total

---

Box 1. Characteristics of the Small Enterprise Sector in Russia

---

Definition of small business. The Law on State Support of Small Entrepreneurship in the Russian Federation[12] defines small businesses as (1) individual entrepreneurs (sole proprietors), (2) farm enterprises, and (3) small enterprises registered as legal entities. These entities are also further defined in terms of the maximum number of their employees: 100 in industrial production, civil engineering or transport; 60 in agriculture; 30 in retail trade or consumer services; and 50 in other sectors or types of business.[a]

Sole proprietors are the preferred form of business and dominate the sector. Businesses registered as legal entities and sole proprietors can take advantage of simplified taxation rules available to small companies.[b] In addition, sole proprietors benefit from a simplified and inexpensive registration process. They are clearly the preferred legal form of business in Russia as evidenced by their share of the total number of SMEs. The overall number of small businesses estimated at 5.6 million has been growing primarily through the influx of sole proprietors estimated to be about 4.5 million. The number of small enterprises registered as legal entities has leveled off at about 900,000 for several years since the mid-1990s.

Enterprises prefer to stay small. Entrepreneurs appear to have an incentive to divide their companies into smaller units rather than grow and expand into larger concerns. Remaining small allows them to continue to take advantage of the simplified taxation system and avoid the costly regulatory burden/rent-seeking attention that growing companies may encounter.

Size and sectoral distribution. Small businesses in Russia consist essentially of microbusinesses with less than 10 employees. The sector as a whole and sole proprietors in particular are dominated by companies engaged in trade, kiosks, restaurants, and service businesses.

The level of development of the small business sector varies considerably by region. The distribution of small business across Russian regions is uneven, with about half concentrated in the relatively well-off Central and Northwestern regions.

Early signs of improvement in the business environment. Despite continued difficulties, the government's efforts to ease bureaucratic hurdles for business are starting to show signs of success. A 2003 World Bank–funded survey among 20,000 SMEs in 20 regions showed that, within just six months, the number of official inspections had diminished by 26 percent. The number of licenses necessary to set up a new business was also reduced by 26 percent while the average license term of validity had grown and licenses were granted more rapidly.

a. In general, one of the key basic criteria used to define SMEs is the number of employees. This criterion is also usually supplemented by the value of annual sales or the balance sheet value of assets. OECD defines SMEs as companies with 1–250 employees and turnover of less than €5 million. Some national legislations provide broader definitions. In the United States, Germany, Italy, or France, a company with up to 500 employees is still considered an SME.

b. The Simplified Tax System consolidates five separate taxes into a single payment at a single flat rate.

---

number of small businesses in that region.[13] The analysis revealed the following correlation: (1) the higher the social and economic development level of the region, the higher the share of small enterprises registered as *legal entities;* and, conversely (2) the lower the region's social and economic development level, the higher the share of small enterprises registered as *sole proprietors.*

---

12. Federal Law no. 88-FZ, June 14, 1995.
13. The social and economic status of the regions was assessed on the basis of three indicators:
    (1) Average per capita gross regional product adjusted to the regional purchasing power level
    (2) Comprehensive indicator of the region's social and economic development level calculated according to the methodology of the Ministry of Economic Development and Trade

The prevalence of sole proprietors in low-income regions may be a reflection of the socioeconomic function of self-employment as an income generation or substitution activity for laid-off workers and unemployed individuals. The proportion of "forced" entrepreneurs may be higher in economically depressed areas with high unemployment rates. Forced entrepreneurs opt for sole proprietorship as a form of business and have few incentives to grow beyond a certain size. In better-off regions that may also benefit from a more auspicious business environment, entrepreneurs may have higher incentives to register as legal entities and expand into more formal and eventually bankable businesses. The higher proportion of legal entities in more dynamic regions is also consistent with the "maturing" of firms as a portion of micro-businesses have now grown into small firms.

For sole proprietors, microfinance is often the only possibility to access credit. Demand for microfinance is thus likely to be high in lower-income regions where sole proprietors are the prevalent form of business.

Estimate of Demand for Microcredit

Microfinance developed in Russia primarily around the provision of microcredit to micro-entrepreneurs. Other microfinance services such as savings, insurance, and microleasing—which have been developed in other countries with a more mature microfinance industry—have not yet (or only marginally) been introduced in Russia. Demand surveys and estimates thus typically focus on demand for microcredit.

Preliminary estimates were provided by prior research conducted by the SME Resource Center (2003) under USAID funding in the framework of the Duma–U.S. Congress Joint Working Group on Small Enterprise (see Appendix A).

Other estimates frequently quoted by the Russian Microfinance Center suggest that the potential market for microfinance providers amounts to 2–3 million entities out of 5 million SMEs and that the total demand for microloans amounts to $5–$7 billion.

The Supply Side

Four types of institutions can be broadly distinguished in the global microfinance delivery system (Foster, Greene, and Pytkowska 2003):

- Commercial, state, or rural banks and specialized micro and small business banks. There are typically two categories of banks involved in microfinance: (1) mainstream banks that introduced lending to small and micro-businesses after their inception are commonly referred to as *"downscaling banks"*; and (2) commercial banks that were established from the onset to provide a broad range of products and services primarily to micro and small enterprises are commonly referred to as *"greenfield banks."*
- Specialized credit-only MFIs, which operate usually on a not-for-profit basis and are registered as NGOs, funds, cooperatives, or branches of a foreign NGO.

---

(3) A comprehensive investment environment indicator based on the investment potential and investment risks indicator calculated by the Expert-RA rating agency. (Materials of the Russian SME Observatory Report, SME Resource Center, Moscow, 2002.)

▓ Membership-based organizations, which are established with the aim of providing financial services to their members. These organizations are fully or largely financed from the share capital and savings of their members. Within this category, two types of institutions can be typically distinguished: agricultural/rural credit cooperatives, which provide services primarily to farmers and rural businesses; and credit unions, which are predominantly urban.

▓ State funds, which operate under the auspices of national or local governments and are wholly or largely financed by public money.

Microfinance is a relatively young phenomenon in Russia (if credit cooperatives are excluded) which started to emerge in the 1990s. It developed through all four types of providers described above, albeit with broadly varying scope and outreach performances. With the exception of KMB Bank (a foreign-owned, specialized microfinance bank), Sberbank, and a handful of regional banks, few Russian commercial banks have engaged in microfinance activities or downscaled. On the opposite side of the spectrum, over the past couple of years, credit unions and credit cooperatives (both urban and rural) have experienced a sharp growth in both number of organizations and membership base. The microfinance market also includes a number of NGOs established with the support of international donors and a large number of state funds.

The leading market providers are KMB Bank (by far the largest microfinance lender in Russia), a few NGOs linked with international networks (FORA, FINCA, and RWMN), and credit cooperatives in a few pilot regions (see Box 2).

In the absence of an umbrella microfinance law, each provider operates under the laws and regulations governing its particular legal form of registration.

Box 2. Lending Methodology

Microfinance providers irrespective of their form typically use two traditional methodological models: (1) the group lending model originated by Grameen Bank whereby all group members are responsible for the timely repayment of any loan to any single member of the group, and (2) individual lending.

Regardless of the type of lending, the microfinance lending methodology is based on basic principles of good banking designed to ensure loan quality and high productivity. Because these principles are applied to a different type of client than the traditional clientele of mainstream banks, the methodology is based on a more flexible approach to collateral. Where traditional collateral is not available, microlenders will accept collateral such as family jewelry and other personal belongings. Character analysis is also key as many borrowers do not have a track record. Microfinance lenders also carefully structure loan repayment schedules so that first-time borrowers do not take on more than they can handle. Borrowers are often offered the incentive of a larger loan in the future if they repay their current loan promptly. Finally, microfinance lenders take a strict "zero tolerance" approach to late loan payments, with a payment delay of even one day considered unacceptable. Much emphasis is placed on training clients to be good and disciplined borrowers. To compensate for the small size and high cost of the loans and become financially sustainable, microlenders must ensure high levels of loan officer productivity (that is, high ratios of loans to employee). Loan officers' compensation is thus typically structured to reward portfolio quality (timely repayment) and growth (number of loans).

Source: "Financing Russia's Real Entrepreneurs," Gail Buyske, unpublished manuscript, January 2005.

The following sections provide an overview of key market providers in each category and emerging industry trends. The information presented below draws primarily on published information, existing analytical materials (MFI ratings when available), discussions with microfinance providers, and consultation with donors. It should be noted that only four Russian-based MFIs report to the MIX. There is thus no central source providing standardized information on providers' performance. In 1999, under USAID funding, FINCA conducted a survey of MFI providers in Russia. The purpose of the survey was to develop a catalogue of microfinance organizations providing microloans in amounts of up to $5,000 for entrepreneurial purposes. Sixty eight out of 89 regions were surveyed. The information collected was basic and self-generated by survey respondents.[14] Even with those limitations, it revealed that a large number of organizations of various types was involved in the provision of microfinance services, and that during the period 1998–2000, the number of microloans had increased by a factor of eight.

To generate an updated and comprehensive catalogue of microfinance providers in Russia, in late 2004, the Russian Microfinance Center conducted a market inventory to identify all providers of loans of up to $10,000 and collect standard information on their performance and outreach. Complete survey results are expected to be available in the fall.

---

14. The survey collected the following information: name of organization, legal form; contact information, number of years of operation, average loan maturity, target clients (by business and legal form), sources of microfinance funds, geographical coverage.

CHAPTER 3

Banks and Microfinance

The "Downscaling" and "Greenfield" Models

As noted above, there are typically two types of banks involved in microfinance: (1) mainstream banks (state-owned or commercial), which introduced lending to small and microbusinesses after their inception, are commonly referred to as *"downscaling banks"*; and (2) banks, which were established from the onset to provide products and services primarily to micro and small enterprises, are commonly referred to as *"greenfield banks."*

Downscaling

Downscaling is a process whereby existing mainstream banks enter the microfinance market and target lower-income individuals or smaller businesses. Downscaling may be motivated by several factors, which can apply in combination. It can be introduced by bank management as a new business development strategy in response to competitive pressures from other financial institutions. Banks may also wish to diversify their portfolio and spread their risk through a large number of unrelated businesses. Motivated by potential profits of a new niche, banks may also downscale to emulate successful microfinance institutions that have demonstrated that, under the right circumstances, microfinance can yield high returns on assets. In some cases, downscaling has also been encouraged by governments and donors. For governments and donors driven by a developmental agenda, the downscaling approach has been used as a means of restructuring inefficient state-owned banks and reaching financially underserved segments of the population. It has also been used as a means of rapidly scaling up microfinance by using existing bank networks and retail branches.

The "downscaling" experience varies across regions and within countries. Some banks appear to have successfully developed small-scale financial products and integrated microfinance as their core business activity. The experience of Bank Rakyat Indonesia (BRI),

---

Box 3. Successful Downscaling: BRI (Indonesia), BNB (Brazil), and BAAC (Thailand)

BNB (Brazil). In 1997, encouraged by its new management and by the new attention to microfinance in political spheres within Brazil, Banco do Nordeste do Brasil (BNB), a state-owned development bank with a mandate to promote economic development in the northeastern states, launched a large-scale microfinance program named "CrediAmigo." At end-2001, it served nearly 60 percent of MFI client micro-entrepreneurs and held about 45 percent of their outstanding loans. Today, Credi-Amigo distributes its products through 164 of BNB's 174 branches. By May 2003, CrediAmigo was among the largest MFIs in Latin America, with 123,000 clients and an active portfolio of R$72 million ($24 million equivalent). About 145 of CrediAmigo's 164 branches are operationally sustainable while CrediAmigo has presented positive returns on assets since June 2000. The Credit Amigo program received technical advice from ACCION International and CGAP and was financially supported by the World Bank. CrediAmigo incorporated best-practice principles emerging from successful microfinance institutions in the world. These include: (1) solidarity group lending, (2) targeting the informal sector, (3) charging interest rates high enough to provide a return on assets sufficient to permit financial sustainability, (4) starting with small loan amounts and gradually escalating loan size with repeat loans, (5) amortizing loans regularly, (6) offering incentives for regular repayment through discounts on the last installment, and (7) penalizing borrowers if repayment falls behind schedule. The program also adopted the principles of product differentiation separating its identity from BNB through a separate entrance (or premises) for each branch office. CrediAmigo represents less than 1 percent of BNB's loan assets, and is being managed as an independent profit center with the objective of monitoring progress toward self-sustainability and eventual separation from BNB.[a]

Bank Rakyat (Indonesia). BRI, one of Indonesia's three large state-owned commercial banks, houses the world's largest microfinance network known as the BRI Unit Desa (village units). The Unit Desa system was established in the 1980s to provide agricultural inputs for the cultivation of rice. In the mid-1980s the system, which was experiencing difficulties, was restructured with a focus on profit orientation. New savings and loan products were introduced as well as results-based staff incentives. By August 2004, BRI's branch offices network had expanded to over 4,000 Unit banks and nearly 200 service posts serving 30 million small depositors and 3.1 million borrowers. By end-2004, BRI Unit Desa's outstanding savings and time deposits amounted to $2.9 billion and loans outstanding to $1.9 billion. BRI Unit Desa has been profitable since 1986. In 2003, BRI had the highest return on equity in the Indonesian banking industry, with almost twice the return booked by other domestic banks on average.

BAAC (Thailand). The Bank of Agriculture and Agriculture Cooperatives of Thailand was established in 1996 as a government-owned agricultural development bank. BAAC is considered a good example of a reformed agricultural development bank, by virtue of its enormous outreach. In 2004, 9 out of 10 farming households in Thailand were BAAC clients and the bank had over 2.7 million active borrowers, an outstanding portfolio of almost $6 billion, and over 10 million savings accounts.[b]

a. "Brazil—Access to Financial Services."
b. CGAP Information Note on Microfinance and Rural Finance, January 2004.

Thailand's Bank for Agriculture and Agricultural Cooperatives (BAAC), and more recently, Banco de Nordeste do Brasil (BNB) suggest that, if conditions are appropriate and specific practices are followed, "downscaling" can be a viable and profitable strategy for banks. These examples also suggest that an existing branch network can greatly help the rollout of microfinance products and allow to reach scale rapidly in a cost-effective manner (see Box 3 and Appendix C).

In Eastern Europe and the CIS, downscaling has been primarily driven by donors through credit line support and capacity-building technical assistance.[15] These programs

---

15. EBRD-sponsored downscaling programs were developed in Russia, Uzbekistan, Kyrgyzstan, Ukraine, Belarus, Bulgaria, Latvia, and Lithuania. KfW has also sponsored several downscaling programs including in Ukraine, Former Yugoslav Republic of Macedonia, Romania, and Armenia.

have had mixed results. In Kazakhstan, the downscaling model appears to have worked well. Seven commercial banks including the largest local banks participate in the EBRD-sponsored downscaling program initiated in 1998. By early 2004, partner banks had opened micro and small enterprise lending units in 135 branches and had disbursed over $162 million. By end-2004, the program had about 43,000 outstanding loans. A newly developed profit center accounting method, which is currently being tested, is yielding strong evidence that the micro and small enterprise business has passed the profitability threshold. Partner banks are thus now committing their own funds to the program[16] (see Appendix B).

However, in some other countries including Russia, as will be discussed further down, donor-induced downscaling did not deliver microfinance services on the large scale that had been expected. As of 2002, few of the early participating banks had invested their own capital in downscaling programs (Foster, Greene, and Pytkowska 2003). While an updated assessment may be warranted to assess participating banks' commitment to downscaling today, this has raised the question of sustainability of these programs beyond donor sponsorship.[17] In some instances, banks may have been more motivated by the potential "reputational returns" of being affiliated with a donor program than by developing a lasting small-scale lending business activity. In other cases, participating banks may have been deterred by the high investment cost of maintaining and expanding small business lending facilities and decided to pursue more mainstream business areas with faster and higher profit margins (larger corporates, investment banking, consumer lending, or mainstream small business finance).

Successful downscaling depends on a number of conditions related to both the downscaling institutions themselves (internal) and the environment in which they operate (external). Bank management must be committed to downscaling and ready to induce the required corporate cultural and institutional changes, that is, hire new staff and/or (re)train existing staff, switch from traditional asset-based lending to cash-flow lending, decentralize lending decision making, develop marketing campaigns targeted to smaller clients, develop strong monitoring systems, and learn to maintain good portfolio quality through regular loan officer interface with clients while controlling operating expenses.

Greenfield Microfinance

In addition to downscaling banks, the last decade saw the development of a significant number of new commercial banks specialized in microfinance. In Eastern Europe and the CIS region alone, 10 new microfinance banks founded by multiple foreign shareholders (mostly donors) were established in the last few years.[18]

---

16. Forty percent of the program's small business portfolio is currently being financed by partner banks' own funds.

17. To ensure partner banks' commitment to microfinance, later downscaling programs in the region have been structured in a way that requires participating banks to use their own capital first before donor credit lines are made available.

18. Shareholders typically include EBRD, IFC, KfW, DEG, Soros Foundation, and Commerzbank. IPC (the German Consulting firm providing credit technology support to these new institutions) is also a shareholder in several of these MFIs through its investment subsidiary IMI.

As evidenced by the significant funding contributed by donors, these banks are costly to develop and depend heavily on donor subsidies to start. As in downscaling programs, significant initial investments must be made in the institutional development of a branch and retail network, Management Information Systems, staff training, product development tailored to local demand, and the development of a client base through targeted advertising. However, overall, once established, these banks have been able to develop strong portfolios and achieve growing levels of profitability as demonstrated by their low levels of arrears and write-offs and increasing returns on equity as they mature (see Table 3.1).

Small and Microbusiness Lending in Russia: Why Have Banks Been Absent from the Scene?

In Russia, commercial banks have *thus far* been mostly absent from the scene. Small and microbusiness lending did not develop to any great extent owing to a combination of structural and environmental constraints that have made and continue (although to a lesser extent) to make small business lending unattractive for commercial banks. These factors range from business preferences and lack of resources to inadequate lending environment and credit skills:

> ▓ *Business preferences.* During most of the 1990s, and particularly in the period leading up to the 1998 financial crisis, commercial banks had few incentives to lend to small business. Russian banks have traditionally catered to small groups of industrialists living off a lending portfolio of a small number of high-volume clients. Lending programs for private individuals and small companies require the creation of an expensive retail network and more personnel for branch offices. Most banks thus focused instead on lucrative foreign exchange (FOREX) operations, investments in government securities, and, for many of the so-called pocket banks, provision of treasury-like products to their affiliated owners. Following the 1998 financial crisis, lending to the real sector concentrated around well-established large enterprises involved in extractive industries or trade. While banks are now increasingly moving into consumer lending (see Box 4), they continue to perceive small business lending as high risk.
>
> ▓ *Lack of resources.* The Russian banking sector is small and highly concentrated. Close to half of all Russian banks have less than $10 million in equity. Banks are also highly concentrated in major urban centers and lack sufficient retail infrastructure to reach small and geographically remote clients. In addition, some 40 percent of total deposits and 70 percent of retail deposits are concentrated in Sberbank. The recently adopted Deposit Insurance Law[19] is expected to create competition to Sberbank and draw back in a portion of population savings kept outside of the banking system

---

19. The deposit insurance scheme will provide insurance for up to 100,000 rubles (about $3,500) to individual depositors in qualifying banks.

Table 3.1 Microfinance Banks in Eastern Europe

	Program start date	Deposits ($ million)	Balance sheet data as of end–Dec. 2004						Performance data				
			Number of loans outstanding (Total)	Volume of loans outstanding ($ million)	Average loan size ($)	Arrears > 30 days to present portfolio	Loan loss provisions to present portfolio	Portfolio growth in 2003, %	Portfolio growth in 2004, %	Additional loan loss provisions in Dec. 2004	Return on average assets (RROA) in Dec. 2004	Return on average equity (RROE) in Dec. 2004	Number of loans / Number of staff in Dec. 2004
ProCredit Bank BiH	1997	28.9	20,119	83.7	4,160	0.7%	2.7%	65%	51%	0.7%	2.2%	13.5%	72
ProCredit Bank Albania	1999	160	22,025	108.0	4,902	0.9%	2.3%	251%	84%	0.7%	1.6%	21.8%	60
ProCredit Bank Georgia	1999	34.0	16,680	68.8	4,124	1.8%	3.8%	37%	45%	0.7%	3.5%	17.9%	31
ProCredit Bank Kosovo	1999	423	29,907	149.9	5,012	0.4%	2.3%	151%	80%	0.4%	1.4%	32.5%	77
ProCredit Moldova	2000	0	5,779	12.6	2,185	0.7%	3.1%	140%	93%	1.7%	1.5%	26.5%	50
ProCredit Bank Romania	2002	34.6	12,250	70.6	5,762	0.3%	1.4%	97%	166%	1.0%	-0.1%	-0.5%	46
ProCredit Bank Ukraine	2001	35.1	21,976	101.3	4,609	0.9%	2.8%	56%	72%	1.2%	1.8%	10.2%	26
ProCredit Bank Serbia	2001	127	37,465	166.2	4,437	0.8%	2.1%	126%	75%	1.4%	0.0%	0.5%	65
ProCredit Bank Bulgaria	2001	103	28,490	190.0	6,669	0.7%	1.6%	244%	89%	1.4%	2.9%	23.1%	46
ProCredit Bank Macedonia	2003	16.1	7,406	32.4	4,369	0.6%	3.5%	—	245%	4.2%	-0.8%	-2.8%	45
Average		96.2	20,210	98.3	4,623	0.8%	2.6%			1.3%	1.4%	14.3%	52

— . Not available.
Source: Authors, based on data from ProCredit Holding published at http://www.procredit-holding.com.

since the 1998 financial crisis. However, at present, most Russian banks and in particular smaller regional banks lack on-lending resources.[20]

■ *Statutory requirements by the Bank of Russia (CBR) and collateral issue.* Collateral is the main criteria for loan loss reserve. Given poor enforcement of property rights, high cost of collateral recovery, and the absence of an effective market for liquidation of seized collateral, banks impose high collateral requirements in anticipation that recovered items may only be realized at a fraction of their value. In addition, CBR imposes tight collateral requirements. Loan classification practice in Russia is formula driven. Until recently, according to CBR's instruction 62-A on loan classification, loans were classified into four categories (standard, substandard, doubtful, and loss), according to the timeliness of payment, the number of times a loan was rolled over, and the quality of collateral. Qualitative judgment on the potential impairment of a borrower was not taken into consideration (see detailed description in Appendix I). In March 2004, CBR replaced instruction 62-A with a new instruction moving the loan classification requirements closer to international standards and allowing provisioning on the basis of risk assessed on a group of loans rather than requiring separate provisioning for each individual loan.[21] Although the new approach may help ease small business lending, it is expected to come into force gradually as banks develop the required capacity and has thus not yet been tested.

■ *Inadequate capacity/lending methodology/lack of skills.* Russian commercial banks regard small business lending as a high-transaction-cost and high-risk business. Many enterprises suffer from poor corporate governance and tend not to report their real financial performance. Banks must thus rely on their own analysis of borrowers' creditworthiness and integrity. However, commercial banks in Russia often lack adequate operational systems and procedures to properly assess risks and customize financial products to the needs of small business clients.

■ *Ineffective lending environment.* While most lending is asset based, the legal and infrastructure environment for collateral remains inefficient. However, draft legislation to develop a modern system of registration of pledged movable property is currently under consideration. In addition, a system of credit bureaus has recently started to develop.[22]

As a result, few Russian commercial banks have engaged in microfinance activities or downscaled.

---

20. According to a recent nationwide public opinion poll conducted (by VTsIOM) in Russia, 70 percent of the adult population has not "banked" since prior to the 1998 financial crisis. When asked what they do with their cash, 38 percent of the people said that they keep it at home (of those, almost two-thirds in foreign currency). Thirty-five percent invest in real estate; Sberbank was the safe-keeper of choice for 27 percent of the respondents while private domestic banks were trusted by only 2 percent and foreign banks by 6 percent. Four percent reported investing in the stock market and 7 percent in jewelry and antiques (Perttunen 2004).

21. CBR regulation 254.

22. Two credit bureaus were recently established: the *National Bureau of Credit Histories,* owned by 12 Russian Banks, the Association of Russian Banks (ARB), TransUnion, and CRIF; and the *Experian-Interfax Bureau of Credit Histories,* in which 20 banks agreed to participate. In addition, on June 10, Sberbank Chairman Andrei Kazmin announced that Sberbank would create its own credit bureau.

To date, banks involved in microlending have thus been primarily limited to those banks which participate in the EBRD-sponsored downscaling program.

EBRD's Russia Small Business Fund—A Donor-Sponsored Downscaling Program

Similar to small business funds developed by EBRD in other CIS countries, the Russia Small Business Fund (RSBF) was established in the mid 1990s to finance micro and small enterprises and strengthen the lending capacity of Russian partner banks. The program provides funds directly to Russian partner banks (for a period of three to five years), which, in turn, make loans to micro and small enterprises at market rates.

The program, which was originally due to close in 2004 and recently extended through 2010, seeks to serve a market segment underserved by commercial banks, with loan size ranging from $20 to 200,000. However, 80 percent of the partner banks' outstanding portfolio is composed of small loans under $10,000 and 60 percent of the loans are under $5,000. The bulk of the portfolio is in working capital loans to sole proprietors for inventory purchase. Since inception, the program disbursed over 182,000 subloans to micro and small enterprises totaling about $1.55 billion in 130 cities.

Participating banks use specific credit assessment procedures and information technology systems created or adapted to meet the processing, information, and reporting requirements of SME lending. The credit assessment procedures are based on cash flow analysis, strong portfolio monitoring where arrears are pursued early and aggressively, and a flexible approach to collateral with emphasis on any possession that has value to its owner (in money or sentimental terms). The methodology is also based on the traditional scaled lending model of microfinance where first-time borrowers receive small short-term amounts that increase over time with the borrower's proven repayment track record.

Up to 2001, at different stages, about 21 domestic banks had participated in the program including all of the major banks with nationwide branch networks.[23] However, the financial sector crisis created massive financial and operational difficulties for many of the participating banks. To ensure orderly loan repayments, EBRD thus transferred the loan contracts that had been seized from failing banks to the Russian Project Finance Bank, in which it was the leading shareholder. The bank's shareholding structure was subsequently changed and a specialized microfinance bank, KMB Bank, was established on its basis. KMB Bank has since become the program's primary engine of growth.

Today the program works through eight partner banks. In addition to the three banks selected in the precrisis years and KMB Bank, four new regional banks were recently added to the network.[24]

---

23. From 1995 until 1998, the program experienced tremendous growth. By July 1998, a total of 14 participating banks had built up an outstanding portfolio of almost $100 million. All of the major banks with nationwide branch networks had signed up, including SBS-Agro, Mosbusinessbank (acquired by Bank of Moscow just before the financial crisis), Inkombank, and Bank Rossiskiy Kredit.

24. Banks selected in the precrisis years include Sberbank, Far East Bank, and NBD and the four new regional banks selected during 2002–2003 include Chelindbank, Uraltransbank, Sibakadembank, and UralSib Bank.

Although the program resumed its expansion plans, the growth prospects of the down-scaling model may be limited by the number of eligible banks. While eighty percent of the top 200 Russian banks claim having SME lending programs, their actual loan size and target clientele do not fit RBSF's small business lending culture. Few of the larger banks with nation-wide branch networks are willing to make business loans under $10,000. On the other end of the spectrum, the majority of regional banks potentially interested in microlending are too small to qualify.[25]

The results of the downscaling program have thus been mixed. Only a handful of banks participated in the program, limiting its overall outreach. In 2003, EBRD conducted an evaluation of the program, which concluded that, from the prospect of institutional impact, the results of the downscaling approach in Russia had thus far been inconclusive and that, ultimately, the sustainability of the program would need to be assessed against partner banks' interest to remain in this market using their own funds after the program's closure.

KMB Bank—Russia's Foreign-Owned Microfinance Bank

As mentioned above, KMB Bank (Bank Kreditovanye Malovo Bisnesa) was established in 1999 on the basis of the restructured Russian Project Finance Bank. Its founding share-holders originally included EBRD, Soros Economic Development Fund, Stichting Triodos-Doen, and DEG. In April 2005, the Italian commercial bank Intesa purchased a 75 percent share of KMB for $90 million.

Since its establishment, KMB Bank has disbursed over $1 billion in micro and small business loans (see Box 4).

Box 4. KMB Bank's Outreach, Services and Financial Performance

As of end-2004, KMB bank had a total portfolio outstanding of about $261 million in close to 33,800 loans and a geographical network of 7 branches and 44 credit and cash offices in 22 regions ranging from Kaliningrad to Vladivostok. Service outlets are concentrated mostly in urban centers of at least 200,000 inhabitants.

As a full-fledged bank, KMB Bank is able to offer a wider range of financial services in addition to loans, notably transfer and depository services. By end-2004, its client base was composed of 26,644 sole proprietors and 6,080 legal entities on the credit side and 15,030 depositors. The observed growth in credit clients was primarily driven by the sharp increase in borrowing by indi-vidual entrepreneurs, which grew from 6,000 in 2001 to over 26,600 in 2004. The bank continues to cater primarily to sole proprietors. Its target group consists of three types of clients. The first group, constituting over 60 percent of the clients, is involved in retail distribution or some form of basic commerce. The second group, which accounts for 20 percent, is composed of entrepre-neurs who have grown beyond family businesses or are involved in more sophisticated services.

(continued)

---

25. Given the extensive investment in TA and training of staff required to downscale, to ensure impact, RSBF looks for candidate banks that have sufficient equity and institutional potential to reach scale. The program relies heavily on donor-funded TA—only a small portion of which is passed on to the banks as a front-end fee. In 2001, for every euro lent through the program about 3 cents were estimated to have been spent in free TA while by end-2002, a total of approximately $76 million had been spent in TA in aggregate terms since Program inception (EBRD 2003).

Box 4. KMB Bank's Outreach, Services and Financial Performance (*Continued*)

The third group, which represents about 18 percent of the clients, is involved in light production and manufacturing sectors. The bank has also recently developed agricultural loans on a pilot basis in Rostov-on-Don and Krasnodar.

Loan product categories are broken down into microcredits ($1,000–30,000), small credits ($30,000–150,000), and medium-size credits ($150,000–500,000). Loans are offered in U.S. dollars, euros, or rubles for maturity terms of up to three years. In number of loans, about 60 percent of the bank's portfolio is composed of loans under $5,000.

As of end-2004, KMB Bank had $335 million in assets. Its credit portfolio increased from $140 million in 2002 to $242 million in 2004. Arrears over 30 days were at 0.76 percent in 2004—a level consistent with the average of the microfinance banks in Eastern Europe. Return on assets went from 1 percent in 2002 to 2 percent in 2003 and 2004 (compared to 2.6 percent in 2003 on average in the Russian banking sector as a whole). Return on equity increased from 15 percent in 2002 to 30 percent in 2003 and 24 percent in 2004 (compared to an average of 17.8 percent in the Russian banking sector in 2003). Net profit increased from $1.5 million in 2002 to $5.3 million in 2004.

Looking Forward: Early Signs of Market-Driven Downscaling

Despite the general low level of small business lending outside donor-sponsored programs, some precursory signs of downscaling have recently been observed.

In January 2004, following a meeting with President Putin, the head of Russia's second-largest state-owned bank, Vneshtorgbank (VTB), announced that VTB would lend $1 billion to small and medium-size businesses in 2004.

While the announcement may have been interpreted as somewhat politically motivated given President Putin's emphasis on the need to nurture small business, in July 2004 VTB launched a brand new small business lending program. The program, which is being rolled out simultaneously in 12 regional branches, offers two products targeted at sole proprietors and businesses with up to $3 million in revenues.[26] These products include microcredits of up to $30,000 (to be processed within three days of the loan application) and business development credits of up to $1 million for both working capital and capital investment.

Given the recent launch of the program, it is still too early to assess its results. However, it should be noted that the program has been designed by KMB Bank-trained staff recently recruited by VTB and is thus based on similar technology which has played a critical role in the former's success.[27]

Anectodal evidence suggests that VTB's growing interest in small business is not an isolated case. Several NGO MFIs and credit unions reported encountering increased competition from local banks as these banks, which are also facing growing levels of competitive pressure, are now looking to develop new business niches.

The recent boom in consumer lending also illustrates a growing trend toward downscaling. Russian commercial banks, encouraged by the oil-driven influx of liquidity in the

---

26. Moscow, St. Petersburg, Nizhni Novgorod, Yaroslavl, Belgorod (Western Russia), Ekaterinburg (Urals), Samara, Voronezh, Rostov-on-Don (Southern Russia), Kranoyarsk, Tomsk (Siberia), and Khabarovsk (Far East).

27. During a recent World Bank Access to Finance conference organized in the Southern Okrug (Sochi, April 2005), local banks reported that VTB became a strong competitor in the small business lending market immediately after the program's launch in January 2005.

economy and increase in population real cash income, have been moving aggressively into retail lending. Lending to "natural persons" as reported by CBR increased by 111 percent from January 2003 to January 2004 (see box 5).

Box 5. Consumer Lending

Growth in consumer lending. Increasing household incomes and consumption levels combined with decreasing margins on corporate loans prompted Russian banks to turn to consumer lending. Personal loans typically include consumer loans, car loans, and mortgage loans. To estimate the size of the consumer loan market by category, analysts group loans by maturity. Loans under three years are used as a proxy for consumer loans and car loans while loans over three years are used as a proxy for mortgage loans. Real consumer loans typically include express loans for household appliance purchases, personal loans, and credit card loans. These loans are usually less than one year in maturity.

Size and growth dynamics. According to CBR, retail loans more than doubled in 2003, growing from Rub 142 billion at the end of 2002 to Rub 300 billion by end 2003. In relative size, retail lending grew from 9.8 to 11 percent of all commercial lending. Twenty-five percent of all retail loans are less than one year to maturity, 20 percent are between one and three years to maturity, and 55 percent are over three years.

Main providers. Until recently, Russian retail banking was almost exclusively dominated by Sberbank. However, starting 2000–2001, a number of other Russian banks began to move into the short-term consumer lending segment of the market. Ruski Standard and Pervoyo OVK were the first two to launch mass-scale consumer loan programs. Sberbank still accounts for 48 percent of all retail lending, however, with 75 percent of its retail portfolio consisting of loans over three years. Consumer loan products include express credits in stores, short-term cash loans, and credit card loans. Although banks are expanding their client base, most primarily cater to middle- and upper-class households.

Rates. Despite declining interest rates, consumer loan rates remain high while corporate loan rates are declining owing to increased competitive pressures and access of Russian corporations to international capital markets. In 2003, average personal loan rates fluctuated between 15 and 24 percent, while corporate loan rates declined from 15–16 percent to 12 percent. Average rates on retail loans under one year ranged from 15 to 30 percent while average rates on corporate loans of the same maturity ranged from 9 to 20 percent. The average premium paid on consumer loans in comparison with corporate loans ranges from 6 to 10 percent depending on the loan maturity, suggesting that small entrepreneurs financing their business via consumer loans pay a premium of 6–10 percent over corporate loan rates.

While the observed surge in lending to "natural persons" reflects a strong increase in pure retail lending (household goods, car loans, mortgages), it may also reflect a disguised increase in small business lending.

Russian individual entrepreneurs use consumer credits to finance their business needs. When borrowing money for their businesses, they tend to borrow as individuals rather than opening a business account. As the only loan category for lending to individuals is "consumer loans," their loans are booked and reported as consumer loans—a practice that has allowed RSBF partner banks to disburse small and microloans reasonably quickly and without incurring prohibitive cost for loan loss provision. As a result, KMB Bank appears fifth in ranking by volume of consumer lending while it is primarily engaged in small business lending. Interestingly, among the top 30 consumer lending banks, five are EBRD partner banks. By virtue of their affiliation to the EBRD program, a portion of their retail portfolio can thus be likewise assumed to consist of business loans to sole proprietors booked as consumer loans.

Although impossible to assess from available data, this may suggest a more general trend. As noted above, the Central Bank has recently simplified its statutory requirements for small business lending. Should a portion of the observed surge in consumer lending reflect an increase in small business lending, the simplified requirements, once brought into practice, may thus lead to an increase in reported small business lending at the expense of retail lending.

Key Observations

- *Few Russian banks are organizationally geared toward micro and small enterprise lending.* This may reflect the initial investment required in setting up retail branch networks to reach small clients, the inability of banks to pass cost-effective adequate judgment on the quality of credits (leading to the perpetuation of an asset-based lending culture), the high regulatory cost related to small loans, and the banks' difficulties to secure acceptable and liquid collateral. SME lending thus continues to a large extent to be perceived by banks as a high-risk and high-cost activity.

- *Improvements in the lending environment have been slow to come.* CBR has been trying to simplify its statutory requirements. However, the new requirements are yet to translate to higher levels of small business lending. In addition, the legislation on the planned collateral registry of movable property is still under development. At the same time, credit bureaus have started to develop. It will be interesting to monitor the impact of these new institutions on the volume of small business lending.

- *While the greenfield microfinance model has been quite successful, the jury is still out on the downscaling model.* KMB Bank has developed a large market outreach and reached increasing levels of profitability. The donor-driven and subsidy-intensive downscaling model, however, has not delivered the expected scale and outreach. The success of the program will be ultimately determined by participating banks' interest in remaining in this niche beyond donor sponsorship.

- *EBRD's microfinance program serves the high end of the micro and small enterprise market* and provides larger loans to larger businesses than other MFIs do. RSBF borrowers tend to be established, urban-based entrepreneurs who have been in business for three years or more. They are mostly traders, that is, passive acquirers of goods for resale. As the lending methodology used under RSBF is based on credit history, heavy emphasis is also placed on repeat borrowers.

- *The recent boom in consumer lending may also reflect an increase in small business lending.* Banks, which are facing increased competitive pressures, are moving aggressively into the consumer lending market. However, a portion of the reported consumer loans may in reality be micro-enterprise loans booked as personal loans, which would reflect a growing trend toward market-driven (versus donor-driven) downscaling in the commercial banking sector.

CHAPTER 4

Credit Cooperatives

Credit Cooperatives—A Solidarity-Based Financial Model

Membership-based organizations that are established with the aim of providing financial services to their members play an important role in many countries. These organizations, often referred to as financial cooperatives, are fully or largely financed from the share capital and savings of their members and are owned and governed by their members. The two basic types of financial cooperatives are agricultural (or rural) credit cooperatives, which provide services primarily to farmers and rural businesses, and credit unions, which are predominantly urban based. To date, credit unions have been established in 84 countries around the world and unite some 123 million members.[28]

Credit cooperatives form an integral part of developed countries' financial systems. In advanced market economies such as the United States, Canada, France, Spain, Germany, and Nordic countries, the process of credit cooperative system development began by setting up a network of primary grassroots-level institutions based on individual membership to address the needs of local communities. Their growth led to the formation of regional credit institutions serving the credit and financial requirements of primary member cooperatives. Further evolution entailed the establishment of national credit cooperative institutions, including large banks. Credit cooperatives that, in some countries, benefited from access to liquidity facilities, deposit insurance, and credit bureaus reached significant scale. For example, the Desjardins movement of Credit Unions is the leading financial institution in Quebec (Canada), where it serves virtually every citizen of the province—issuing 36 percent of consumer loans, 39 percent of mortgages, over 23 percent of commercial loans, and 42 percent

---

28. WOCCU.

of agricultural loans and mobilizes about 45 percent of all savings deposits.[29] Credit unions have also emerged as the single most important source of credit to micro-enterprises in Latin America, providing $2.6 billion in loans to micro-enterprises.

Credit cooperatives have a deep rooted history in Eastern Europe. Community-based financial institutions have had one of the longest legacies in Central and Eastern Europe, where the original German-born Raiffeisen model of savings and loan cooperatives started spreading in the late 1800s. In Russia, by 1916, credit cooperatives (both urban and rural) had 14 million members.

During the Soviet period, credit unions ceased to exist as separate legal entities and were transformed into mutual assistance funds (the so-called *Kasas Vzoimno pomoshi*), which no longer operated as independent, community-based institutions. They were managed instead by state-owned companies and trade unions, which provided operational cost subsidies. Savers were no longer remunerated and borrowers were granted interest-free loans.

In the early 1990s, following the fall of communism, member-owned and member-managed savings and credit institutions reemerged in their original form. The Polish credit union movement is considered one of the most successful and sophisticated in the region. Since its rebirth 13 years ago the movement has expanded rapidly, and today unites over 1 million members. Its total assets increased from an initial Zl 4 million to 3, 5 billion ($0.9 billion). Credit unions in Poland offer a wide variety of services comparable to those of commercial banks, including term deposits, savings accounts, short-term instant loans, long-term housing loans, money transfers, ATM services, electronic payments of monthly bills, insurance services, and pension funds products (see Appendix D).

In some countries, the revitalization of the credit-union movement was actively supported by WOCCU[30] and Développement International Desjardins (DID). The World Council of Credit Unions has notably been instrumental in developing commercially oriented operating guiding principles and a system to monitor and evaluate the financial performance of credit unions (PEARLS).[31]

Credit Cooperatives in Russia: A Recent Accelerated Growth Despite a Lacking Legal and Regulatory Environment

In Russia, the reemergence of credit cooperatives has been largely grassroots driven. In 1991, the confederation of consumer rights lobbied for the right of citizens to form credit

---

29. DID Project in Russia, Vladislav Krivosheev, May 2005.

30. WOCCU recently completed a technical assistance project in Ecuador. The project, which was designed to strengthen credit unions, worked with 23 credit unions and supported the Superintendency of Banks on regulatory reforms. Technical assistance included development of standardized operating procedures, strengthened financial discipline through introduction of the PEARLS monitoring system, annual business and marketing plans, revised credit policies and procedures, and new savings and loan products. During 1996–2003, savings in the supported credit unions increased from about $60 million to over $200 million; loans increased from $75 million to over $200 million; assets grew from $114 million to almost $300 million; and delinquency rates decreased from 17.5 percent to below 6 percent. In addition, between 1996 and 2001, membership increased by almost 350,000.

31. PEARLS, which includes 45 financial ratios, stands for Protection, Effective financial structure, Asset quality, Rates of return and costs, Liquidity, and Signs of growth.

unions based on the original model, which would allow people to protect their savings against inflation.

However, early grassroots initiatives were not given strong government support and did not translate into a sound and steady development of the sector. The development of credit cooperatives was held back by the lack of recognition at the policy level of the importance of cooperative credit, notably for small business development. Lawmakers also feared a return of the financial pyramid schemes that had multiplied in the early 1990s (for example, see Box 6 for a summary of the MMM scandal).

This lack of support and understanding of the potential role of credit cooperatives resulted in a slow-developing and fragmented legal and regulatory framework, as well as a supervisory vacuum.

Fragmented Legal Framework

In the absence of a clear framework law, the cooperative sector is governed by several legislative acts adopted over time that pertain to different types of cooperatives. Credit cooperatives are essentially regulated by four pieces of legislation: the Civil Code (Article 116); the Law on Agricultural Cooperatives (December 8, 1995); the Law on Consumer Cooperatives (consumer societies and their unions) (July 11, 1997); and the Law on Consumer Credit Cooperatives of Citizens (August 7, 2001). In practice, three broad types of cooperatives have emerged under the existing legal framework:

- *Agricultural credit cooperatives,* which specialize in the provision of savings services and business loans to their members, comprising individuals or legal entities— typically farmers and agricultural producers
- Consumer credit *cooperatives of citizens* (credit unions), whose membership is restricted to physical persons and which provide loans to their members for business and/or consumer purposes
- *Consumer cooperatives* (mutual credit societies), which, unlike citizens' cooperatives, can include both physical and legal entities and provide loans to their members for business and/or consumer purposes

---

Box 6. The MMM Pyramid Scheme

In the early 1990s, the incomplete legal and regulatory framework allowed a number of fly-by-night companies to arise and take advantage of legal loopholes to set up speculative schemes. The most infamous was the MMM Corporation, a large-scale pyramid scheme set up to defraud millions of Russian citizens of their savings. MMM was established in 1991 by Sergey Mavrodi. In 1994, the company started issuing investment certificates offering 10 to 20 percent weekly return. MMM embarked on a very aggressive populist marketing campaign: it ran commercials on state television channels during primetime, paid for all-day free travel on the Moscow metro, sponsored the Russian soccer team during the 1994 World Cup, and published full-page ads in *Pravda* and *Izvestia.* By July 1994, between 5 to 10 million people had invested some 10 trillion rubles ($1.7 billion) in the MMM scheme. Finally, in late July 1994, the Ministry of Finance issued a statement warning the public about the nature of the MMM Corporation. This statement caused a first investors' run on the corporation, which triggered the eventual collapse of the original scheme in October 1994. MMM was declared bankrupt only in 1997 by a Moscow arbitration court.[a]

a. Peter Symes, 2004 (http://www.pjsymes.com.au/articles/MMM.htm).

Key differences among the various forms of cooperatives lie primarily in authorized membership profile and ceiling and authorized services to members. Membership organizations have tended to register under one law or another largely depending on the law's degree of flexibility rather than the nature of their underlying activity. In addition, the evolutionary nature of the legal framework resulted in some confusion among the different types of cooperatives. A number of cooperatives that were established before the adoption of the Law on Citizens Cooperatives (credit unions) continue to operate under the Law on Consumer Cooperatives and/or the Civil Code whereas, to reflect the actual nature of their activities, they should have reregistered under the Law on Citizens Cooperatives.

A "framework law" on credit cooperatives was introduced in the Duma in 2002 but has been stalled since first reading. Industry lobbyists are pushing for the adoption of this new law, which is expected to ease the development of the sector by providing a clear and consistent harmonized legal framework and by removing current restrictions imposed on membership size (currently capped at 2,000) and target use of credit.

Absence of a Supervisory Framework

In Russia, credit cooperatives are not subject to external supervision. Supervision is generally conducted internally in accordance with the rules and procedures stipulated in individual cooperatives' charter documents. The Law on Agricultural Cooperatives is more prescriptive in this area because it specifies that agricultural cooperatives that belong to a federative association (union) are subject to audits executed by the association. The frequency and scope of these audits are defined in the associations' internal rules. However, since membership in these associations is voluntary, only those agricultural cooperatives that are members of an association are subject to this form of external supervision.

At the annual microfinance conference organized by the Russian Microfinance Center (RMC) in December 2003, the Ministry of Finance (MOF) announced that it had been entrusted with the responsibility of regulating and overseeing credit unions' activities and that the government would issue a regulation amending the MOF's statute to add this regulatory and supervisory function to its duties. The MOF emphasized that it intended to be "light-handed" in its regulation of the sector and would first focus on citizens cooperatives (credit unions) and start by addressing three areas: (1) preparing a charter template and writing nonprudential guidelines, which cooperatives would be required to reflect in their by-laws; (2) establishing the amount of required loan loss reserves; and (3) developing reporting indicators. The MOF also announced that a central filing body would be set up and that it would develop a one-stop-shop registration system in cooperation with the Tax Ministry.

Follow-up implementation arrangements to this effect have not yet been finalized and the supervisory framework for credit unions appears to remain under discussion. The issue of supervisory responsibility for rural credit cooperatives is even more undefined as no government agency has formally been designated to oversee rural cooperatives.

Although still slow and largely underdeveloped, notably by contrast with those of neighboring countries such as Poland and Romania, the Russian credit cooperative sector experienced significant growth in the last five years in both numbers and membership size. In 2004, there were 703 agricultural cooperatives (compared to 42 in 1998) and 540 citizens and consumer cooperatives (compared to 143 in 1998; see Table 4.1).[32]

---

32. As legal entities, all credit cooperatives must register with the Ministry of Justice and tax authorities. However, no licensing system for credit cooperatives has been developed yet. In the rural credit coop-

Table 4.1 Credit Cooperatives' Growth (1998–2004)					
		1998	2000	2003	2004
Agricultural credit	Total number	42	122	530	703
cooperatives	Total membership	839	6,838	41,618	70,843
	Average membership	20	56	78	100
Citizens cooperatives	Total number	143	200	440	540
and consumer	Total membership	33,226	48,000	222,686	350,000
cooperatives	Average membership	232	240	506	648

Source: Authors, based on information received from URCC, RCCDF and the League of Credit Unions.

Given the recent accelerated growth, developing an adequate regulatory and supervisory framework for both credit unions and rural credit cooperatives will thus be a critical undertaking.

In designing a regulatory and supervisory framework, the Government will need to consider and weigh the following: (1) how to introduce prudential and nonprudential guidelines that would ensure the sound development of the sector and protect the growing number of member depositors without suffocating the industry; and (2) which level and model of supervision to select, taking into account the current capacity of supervisory authorities and potential for industry self-regulation. In recent years, many countries have tackled this issue, in some instances with the help of donors. The Government of Russia will thus be able to draw from the large body of knowledge and experience accumulated in this area (see Box 7).

Box 7. Basic Models of Regulation and Supervision of Credit Cooperatives

Cooperative financial institutions (CFIs) can provide a variety of financial services including savings (that is, redeemable resources from members or from the public) and credits. Understanding the potential role of CFIs in providing access to financial services to the underserved, supervisory authorities and industry providers have worked together to develop adequate and conducive regulatory frameworks focusing on prevention (governance and prudential criteria), control (inspection, internal and external audit), and protection (deposit insurance scheme, security funds within the organization).

Differentiating between nonprudential regulation and prudential regulation and supervision is key to developing an appropriate regulatory and supervisory framework. Nonprudential regulation measures such as registration procedures, externally audited reports, standardized accounting, and financial reports can be used to set industry standards and develop the CFI sector in an

---

(continued)

---

erative sector, estimates can be obtained from two federal and closely intertwined "Apex" institutions (second-tier or wholesale organizations that channel funding)—the Union of Rural Credit Cooperatives (URCC) and the Rural Credit Cooperatives Development Foundation (RCCDF). Established in 1997, these dominate the sector. Data on credit unions is available from the League of Credit Unions, which was established in 1994 and comprises 153 credit unions.

Box 7. Basic Models of Regulation and Supervision of Credit Cooperatives (*Continued*)

---

orderly fashion. Prudential regulation and supervision entails licensing, compliance with prudential standards, off-site and on-site supervision, and sanctions—given that the licensing authority vouches for the soundness of the financial institution.

Regulatory frameworks should set out clear guidelines dealing with governance and administration, credit and supervisory committees, levels of capital requirements and reserves, internal audits, accounting, reporting, dissolution and liquidation procedures, and prevention of conflicts of interest. Some countries specify capital requirements for CFIs that are authorized a higher level of operation (such as receiving deposits from nonmembers) and require CFIs to maintain solvency ratios equal to or above the 8 percent required for banks as per the international Basel I standards.

Supervisory frameworks vary widely across countries depending notably on the level of development of the sector and capacity of the supervisory authorities. In general, supervision of CFIs differs from supervision of banks because CFIs are often geographically dispersed, have small membership, represent a small share of the financial market, and pose a limited systemic risk to the economy. Given the cost of supervision for both the CFIs and the supervisory body, one issue that has also emerged is whether all CFIs need to be supervised or whether there should be a maximum asset- size over which a CFI should be supervised. The three commonly observed methods of supervision are direct, delegated, and self-regulation.

Direct supervision (both on-site and off-site supervision), which is conducted by an independent superintendency or by the central bank. Although this may be the first best approach to supervision, it is not economically viable in most countries and places a high burden on the designated supervisory body. Some countries, such as Bolivia, have opted to supervise only credit unions of a certain asset size.

Delegated supervision, where the superintendency or central bank fully delegates supervisory functions—including interventions and sanctions—to a private agent such as a federation of credit cooperatives. Responsibility for establishing prudential regulations usually remains with the superintendency. Delegated supervisory agents could also be an entity fully independent of credit unions or two or more regional credit union federations specializing in supervision (the German model). Both still require overall superintendency or central bank oversight. Low levels of federation and cohesion of the industry (absence of federations with sufficient coverage of the sector) can constrain the effectiveness of delegated supervision. Effective delegated supervision also requires the system to be made financially viable using mechanisms such as user fees. A variation of delegated supervision is the auxiliary supervision model whereby the private agent undertakes the supervisory role but sanctions remain the responsibility of the superintendency. Mexico is developing its CFI regulatory framework along the lines of this model.

Self-regulation, whereby a federation of cooperatives performs certain control functions of its members based on a regulatory framework and monitoring process voluntarily accepted by the cooperatives. Self regulation has worked well in developed countries such as Canada (DID) and the Netherlands (Rabo Bank), where discipline and compliance with fiduciary requirements among network members have been high. One of the main weaknesses of this model is the potential conflict of interest that can arise in a federation undertaking both the development and capacity building role for the CFI sector alongside supervisory functions.

Source: Proceedings of the World Bank Workshop on Cooperative Financial Institutions, June 2004.

Rural Credit Cooperatives—The Only "Game in the Village"?

Commercial banks are scarce in rural areas and play a marginal role in small towns. Over 80 percent of all bank assets are concentrated in Moscow or the Moscow region while Sberbank reportedly continues to withdraw from loss-making rural areas and small towns, closing 71 branches in 2002 alone. The Russian agricultural state-owned bank, Rosselkhozbank (established in June 2000 to replace the defunct Russian agricultural bank, SBS Agro) and Rosagroleasing mainly serve the agro-industrial complex dominated by former collective farms converted into agro-holdings. Commercial banks operate only in large cities and state-controlled banks present in the countryside are not well suited to deal with numerous small borrowers. Thus, for small clients such as household plot holders, family farming businesses, and nonagricultural small-scale enterprises in rural areas, rural credit cooperatives are often the only channel to access credit. The development of Rural Credit Cooperatives (RCCs) has therefore emerged in response to the unavailability of formal financial services and as a complement to the banking sector in rural areas. (See box 8.)

The recent growth in rural credit cooperatives has also been facilitated by the introduction of the federal Law on Agricultural Cooperatives in 1995. Almost all RCCs are registered under this law. Despite remaining deficiencies,[33] with the recent amendments passed by the Duma in June 2003, the law has provided the basic legal foundation for the initial development of a multitier national system of RCCs:

■ *First-tier RCCs.* Although still small, the number of RCCs grew from 17 in 1997 to 703 in 2004, with total membership exceeding 70,000 and about $42,4 million in aggregate credit portfolio. As a rule, RCCs are most developed in regions where a high proportion of family farming businesses coincide with a below-average banking infrastructure. Although RCCs have been established throughout Russia, they have

---

Box 8. Rural Credit Cooperatives' Clients

◆ Part-time *household plot holders,* growing vegetable for their own needs and for local markets. Many families' own consumption depends on their household plot production. Household plot holders have been estimated to include about 12 million households. Household plots' share of Russia's overall agricultural production has also been growing significantly since the transition and reached 54 percent in 2000. In 2002, with only 6 percent of agricultural land, household plots accounted for close to 90 percent of potato production, over two-thirds of vegetable, and over half of milk, livestock, and poultry production. Loans are mainly used for gardening tools and materials, seeds, pesticides, and fertilizers.

◆ A second, more distinct group is composed of approximately 260,000 *family farming businesses* with an average of 52 ha of land. Loans are used for purchase of fuel and oil materials, animals, mechanical tools, and spare parts.

◆ A third category is composed of *nonagricultural SMEs* in rural areas and small towns. By conservative estimates, this category would include some 84,000 clients. Owing to the availability of mostly short-term loans, nonagricultural SMEs are concentrated in the service sector and loans are typically disbursed to hairdressing salons, laundries, cafes, shoe repair shops, and clothing workshops. Small production and processing businesses include meat processing, bakeries, mills, and dairies.

Source: Microfinanza rating report of RCCDF, 2004.

---

33. Under the current law, only agricultural producers are allowed to become members of a rural credit cooperative. This restriction does not jibe with the diversity of rural communities.

developed most intensively in the Volgograd, Rostov, and Saratov regions, which benefited from early donor support.[34] Typical loan amounts vary from about $300 to 3,000, with a maturity of up to one year. Annual interest rates on loans given out by RCCs vary by region and by type of product but, overall, tend to range from 30 to 60 percent. Legal entities (usually private farms) tend to prevail among founders in RCCs' initial years of development. Over time, as RCCs mature and expand, they become attractive to a wider range of the rural population and experience a shift in membership profile and activity focus. They tend to include a larger number of plot holders and sole proprietors only indirectly related to agricultural production (processing, trade, marketing, services), and their activities tend to broaden beyond the initial agrarian focus (see Table 4.2 on RCC trends).

▨ *Second-tier RCCs.* Regional second-tier credit cooperatives have also been established in several regions. Second-tier RCCs were set up to redistribute excess liquidity among their member first-tier RCCs and to attract external resources on behalf of their members. They also typically act as the main, regional groups that lobby the government for support and provide training services.

▨ *The Rural Credit Cooperatives Development Fund (RCCDF).* RCCDF was registered in February 1997 as a nonprofit Apex institution providing financial, methodological, and advocacy support to rural credit cooperatives. In 1999, RCCDF received a $6 million grant from the U.S. Department of Agriculture (USDA) to refinance accredited RCCs. Forty-five first-tier and two second-tier RCCs have been accredited to date under the program and receive refinancing loans (at 18–22 percent annual interest) from the fund for on-lending to their members.[35] Loans issued to credit cooperatives range from $21,000 to 610,000 and cater primarily to clients involved in agricultural production. About 152 RCCs have benefited from the program to date.

Table 4.2 Rural Credit Cooperatives

	1998	1999	2000	2001	2002	2003	2004
Value of RCC capital (million rubles)	6	9	16	35	79	158	248
Value of loans disbursed by RCCs (million rubles)	15	40	110	350	550	750	1,186
Number of registered RCCs	42	79	122	211	372	530	703
Number of RCC members	839	2,133	6,838	12,205	28,437	41,618	70,843

Source: ACDI/VOCA and RCCDF.

---

34. The Volgograd and Rostov regions emerged as pioneers and were subsequently emulated by other regions including Saratov, Astrakhan, Krasnodar, Orenburg, Adygeya, Tomsk, Chuvashiya, Mari-el, Perm, and Udmurtiya.

35. To be accredited, an RCC must be officially registered, show a track record of at least one full loan cycle with a portfolio at risk over 30 days below 3 percent and a restructured portfolio below 2 percent of loans outstanding, and must have committed local members who have established the RCC with their own start-up capital.

Accredited RCCs represent 81 percent of total RCC assets and operate in 22 of 89 Russian regions. The average disbursed loan under the program is larger than that disbursed by cooperatives using their own funds and amounts to about $5,000 with an average maturity of approximately 12 months. As of May 2005, RCCDF had an active loan portfolio of $8.6 million. To increase its outreach, RCCDF has been exploring possibilities of raising commercial funding and, in March 2004, commissioned a rating by Microfinanza, following which it concluded a first loan agreement with Blue Orchard for $150,000; the loan was fully repaid in January 2005. The German development bank, KfW, also provided important support by funding international audits of RCCDF financial statements and a follow-up rating by Microfinanza in 2005.[36] In order to increase operational efficiency and prepare organizationally for scaling up, RCCDF management, together with 10 RCCs also established a national credit cooperative to act as an Apex with the option of a further transformation into a nonbank credit organization or bank at a later stage.

■ *Union of Rural Credit Cooperatives (URCC).* URCC was set up in 1997 by rural credit cooperatives with the support of RCCDF. It brings together 205 RCCs, which account for approximately 90 percent of the sector in assets and members. Membership in URCC is voluntary. The organization is financed by membership fees, cost-covering fee-based services, and activity-related donor grants. URCC plays an important advocacy role, provides training and consulting services, and publishes *Selski Kredit* (Rural Credit), a monthly journal.

Although still preliminary, the rural credit cooperative sector has started to develop along the lines of a federated system. This is a positive development given that federated networks tend to encourage greater integration through the creation of a shared image, mutual solidarity associated with self-control and discipline, standardized operations, and harmonized internal governance (World Bank 2004b).

In the absence of a clearly identified regulatory framework, the industry has also taken steps toward self-regulation and adoption of prudential norms on a voluntary basis. The recent amendments to the Law on Agricultural Cooperatives specify that all rural credit cooperatives are required to stipulate standard prudential controls in their charters. URCC and RCCDF have thus worked to develop specific prudential norms based on international standards and designed a CAMELS-based rating and monitoring system for RCCs.[37]

As it continues to expand, to ensure strong and sound growth, the RCC sector will need to further address financial and organizational issues such as savings mobilization, access to external refinancing, and development of methodology and technology to support a wider range of products.

---

36. In December 2004, KfW also founded the "GERFO" foundation. GERFO, which was set up with an initial charter capital of $1 million will support rural SMEs engaged in production, services, and trade by providing loans through first-, second, and third-tier RCCs.

37. This system allows RCCDF to assign a rating for each accredited RCC based on an evaluation and rating of six main components of the RCC's financial and operational performance including Capital adequacy, Asset quality, Management quality, Earnings quality and level, Liquidity adequacy, and Sensitivity to market risk.

Credit Unions: From Social Safety Net to Entrepreneurship Support

Urban-based credit unions have also experienced significant growth over the past five years. As did rural credit cooperatives, these unions emerged in response to the lack of availability of formal banking services.

During the difficult years of the transition period, when salaries and pensions were not paid on time, credit unions were an important social safety net and played an income-smoothing role by extending subsistence loans substituting for delayed incomes. Over time, credit unions became important providers of consumer loans and business loans to micro-entrepreneurs.

Credit unions usually have a few large member-savers (depositors) and a large number of small savers. Lower-income members who deposit very small amounts usually make up the majority of credit union membership. However, larger savers, while constituting a small percentage of the total number of clients, tend to contribute the majority of the deposit-base volume. Members have strong incentives to place their savings with credit unions as these institutions pay significantly higher interest rates on deposits than banks.

The majority of credit cooperatives are located in Western Russia. According to the League of Credit Unions, in 2003, four federal districts (Central, Northwestern, Southern, and Volga) collectively accounted for 324 of the 440 credit unions recorded by the League. Donors have played an instrumental role in supporting the early development of the credit union sector, notably in the South.[38]

Membership size, product range, and interest rates vary considerably across board. Average membership size tends to be well below the 2000 cap imposed by the Law on Citizens Cooperatives. However, a few cooperatives such as EKPA in Siberia, which registered in 1993 under the Law on Consumer Cooperatives, have large memberships (22,000 members). Product range also varies considerably. While a growing number of credit unions have recently widened their product range to include new products such as business loans or housing loans, some continue to specialize primarily in consumer loans. Interest rates also vary widely. Data gathered from a sample of six credit cooperatives throughout Russia[39] show that annual interest rates can vary from 18 to 108 percent per annum. Loan sizes observed from the same sample show that loans can range from about $300 to 4,000. Loan sizes and lending terms tend to increase as clients maintain a good track record.

The example of Alternativa (Box 9), a credit union based in Dubna (Moscow region) illustrates well the recent developments observed in the sector and challenges faced by credit unions.

---

38. In early 1999, DID launched a two-phase Canadian International Development Agency (CIDA)-funded project designed to support the development of sound credit unions in pilot Russian regions. Phase 1 tested the DID model of credit cooperative development in the Volgograd region where a network of newly created and existing credit cooperatives was established and received intensive training in the areas of development of new financial products, internal control, management information systems, marketing, and audit. During Phase 2, the program was rolled out to neighboring regions and three additional associations were established (the Altai, Kuzbass, and South-Russia associations). In 2003, these four associations accounted for 95 credit cooperatives with a total membership of over 43,000, total assets of $16,6 million, and total savings of $12,9 million.

39. Data obtained from the League of Credit Unions cover credit unions established from 1993 to 2001 in Amursk, Vladimir, Smolensk, St Petersburg, Lytkarino, and Urai.

Box 9. Alternativa

Alternativa was originally established in 1995 in Dubna as a consumer cooperative under the Consumer Cooperation Law. In 2001, following the adoption of the Law on Citizens Cooperatives, Alternativa reregistered as a citizens' cooperative.

Alternativa, which was established and is being managed by a former Sberbank employee, started off with 15 members and grew by 200 new members a year on average. In its early years of operation, it focused primarily on social loans (education loans to members borrowing as little as $10 to buy textbooks), consumer goods loans (refrigerators, televisions, and so on), and health loans (for instance, dental work). In 1996, in the wake of the pyramid scheme scandals, Alternativa introduced new products such as business loans to attract new members and is now testing additional products such as mortgage and housing improvement loans. Since January 1996, Alternativa has issued 11,000 business loans. Its long-term strategy is to develop a portfolio composed of 50 percent business loans, 30 percent mortgage/housing loans, and 20 percent consumer loans.

Average loan size is $500 for individuals and $1,700 for businesses. All members join and all loans are made on member recommendation. Reported repayment rate is 99 percent.

Alternativa reports facing strong competition from banks—notably Sberbank, Avtobank-Nikoil, MDM Bank, First OVK/ROSBANK Group, and Vozrozhdenye—as the latter offer lower-interest loans. Alternativa sees its comparative advantage in its flexibility, simplified documentation, and fast access. It also offers higher interest rates on savings. In addition to loan and savings products, Alternativa offers marketing support to its members. For example, members who buy services from other member entrepreneurs (such as a hairdresser) receive a discount.

As of end-2004, Alternativa had a total membership of 1,640 people (80 percent women) and Rub 11.4 million in outstanding loan portfolio (about $412,000). Sixty-six percent of the loan portfolio comprised consumer loans, 18.3 percent business loans for entrepreneurial activities, and 15.7 percent mortgage loans. The average member is 45 years old, with a family of four. While it continues to expand (eight new credit unions were recently created in the region based on the same model), Alternativa reported that a number of factors related to legal restrictions and/or capacity shortage have been restricting its operations and limiting its growth. These include (1) the 2,000 cap on membership imposed by law, (2) the inability to lend to legal entities (prohibited by the Law on Citizens Cooperatives), (3) the 50 percent cap on business loans, (4) limited access to external sources of funding, and (5) the high quorum imposed for annual meetings (currently 70 percent of members).

Source: Interview with Alternativa, May 2005.

Key Observations

- *Cooperatives and in particular rural cooperatives have emerged as a complement to the banking sector.* The ongoing retreat of banks from already underbanked rural areas and small communities has deprived increasing numbers of family farms and rural-based entrepreneurs of access to finance. Credit cooperatives have emerged to fill this gap.
- *Although the credit cooperative sector remains small, it has experienced accelerated growth in the past few years.* With about 420,800 members for a population of 144 million, the penetration of cooperative finance is far below 1 percent. In the rural cooperative sector, only 1 out of 1,000 rural inhabitants is a member of a credit cooperative and the amount of credit granted per person in rural areas is less than $1 a year. Yet, despite a slow start, the sector has experienced significant growth over the past few years, albeit starting from a very low point. Since 1998, the number of rural credit cooperatives has increased 16-fold and membership by a factor of 84.

■ *The cooperative sector is unsupervised.* Russian authorities have only recently started to address the issue of regulation and supervision of the cooperative sector; this will be a critical undertaking in light of the recent accelerated growth observed in this sector.

■ *Credit cooperatives in general tend to have small membership.* Average membership for urban-based credit unions was 648 in 2004 and 100 for rural credit cooperatives.

■ *Data available on RCCs show that loan repayment rates are high.* According to RCCDF, RCC on-time repayment rates average 95 percent.

■ *Cooperatives offer a growing range of products.* Cooperatives are increasingly looking to branch out and develop new products such as business loans and mortgage loans in response to market competition and member needs. Some cooperatives, notably in urban areas, report facing steep competition from banks in consumer lending.

■ *Credit cooperatives have limited access to external finance.* The primary source of refinancing for credit cooperatives is the share capital contributed by their members and retained earnings after deductions for loan loss reserves or other reserves. In the most sophisticated regional RCC systems, with Volgograd and Rostov as the frontrunners, savings by members have grown significantly since 2000, albeit from a very modest base.[40] Some cooperatives have also benefited from donor support such as RCCDF's on-lending facility and the TAISP grant facility funded by USAID. While some cooperatives have also been able to secure commercial bank loans, this has remained a marginal trend.

---

40. In Volgograd, in 2004 total loan volume had reached Rub 718 million and total savings Rub 422 million.

CHAPTER 5

Nongovernmental Organizations

Nongovernmental Microfinance Institutions in Russia: A Difficult Start Due to Legal Ambiguities

NGO MFIs are nonprofit nonmembership organizations specialized in the provision of microloans to sole proprietors, small businesses, and individuals for consumer purchases.

NGO MFIs have spearheaded the development of the microfinance industry in many countries of Eastern Europe and Asia. Most were initially established and capitalized by donors. Once established, NGO MFIs emerged as strong industry lobbyists advocating for the recognition of the industry and necessary changes in the legal and regulatory framework and setting best practice industry standards.

Russia's NGO MFIs, most of which were set up under USAID funding, experienced significant difficulties in their early years of operations owing to the legal ambiguities associated with their status and the nature of their activity.

Most NGO MFIs are registered as noncommercial organizations. As such, their operations are governed by the Civil Code and the Law on Noncommercial Organizations.[41] Confusion has arisen from the fact that MFIs operate under the framework of noncommercial

---

41. The Federal Law on Noncommercial Organizations # 7-FZ of January 12, 1996 specifies, among other things, that noncommercial organizations can be established by a single physical or legal person for social, charitable, cultural, educational, or other public good purposes, which must be declared in the organization's charter. It also specifies that noncommercial organizations can engage in entrepreneurial activities, as long as these activities are conducted in pursuit of one of the purposes listed above. Authorized funding sources are listed as founders' contributions, external donations, proceeds from the production of goods and services, dividends from securities, property income, and other income generated from authorized entrepreneurial activities.

organizations but, in fact, carry out quasi-banking commercial activities by lending money and charging interest on their loans.

In the absence of a clear legal framework defining and regulating microfinance activities, the ambiguity in the legislation regarding the legality of credit delivery by nonbank financial institutions has resulted in high legal fees and created operational difficulties for most NGO MFIs. In the early days of NGO microfinance development, legal practitioners in the area of banking law had taken the position that any activity involving the systematic extension of loans was prohibited unless the lender was a bank or a credit organization licensed by the Central Bank (TACIS 2001).

In addition, NGO MFIs had to spend significant time lobbying for changes in the unfavorable fiscal treatment applied to their operations. Until recently, microlending institutions were confronted with a tax regime that put them at a disadvantage compared to banks. While bank operations were exempt from value-added tax (VAT), NGO MFIs (except for those registered as funds) were frequently required to pay VAT.

These legal and taxation issues, which have significant impact on MFI profitability (and therefore sustainability), have been resolved on a case-by-case basis through individual or collective lobbying.

A Wide Range of Programs

The majority of NGO MFIs were set up with the support of donor programs. Several were established under the support or trademark of existing leading international microfinance organizations such as FINCA, Opportunity International, ACDI/VOCA, and Women World Banking. Three of the leading NGO microfinance operations are described below.[42] A detailed program description of other NGO MFIs is also provided in Appendix E.

FORA Fund

FORA Fund was founded by Opportunity International in June 2000 as a noncommercial microfinance organization headquartered in Nizhny Novgorod. It operates through six hubs and 27 satellites, covering 21 regions in Western Russia.[43] FORA primarily caters to low-income microbusinesses and micro-entrepreneurs engaged in retail trade, with a small percentage in wholesale trade, services, and manufacturing. FORA uses both individual lending and solidarity group lending to groups of three to nine individuals. Loans range from $300 to 17,500 for maturity of 1 to 24 months depending on the loan size. The average loan amount is $1,300 for group lending and $1,800 for individual lending. Types of loan security used by FORA include collateral, group, or third-party guarantees. As of end-2004, FORA had about 15,900 active clients. Over 80 percent of its loans are group loans and 75 percent of recipients are women.

---

42. The information provided below (and summarized in Tables 5.1 and 5.2) was compiled using existing information published by individual NGOs, extracted from available rating reports, or collected through interviews with NGO providers and consultation with donors.

43. Geographical coverage includes Belgorod, Volgograd, Voronezh, St. Petersburg, Leningradskaya oblast, Lipetsk, Nizhny Novgorod, Velikiy Novgorod, Rostov-on-Don, Kursk, Vologda, Karelia, Ulyanovsk, Republic of Chuvashiya, Republic of Mariy El, Ryazan, Tula, Pskov, Penza, Tambov, and Saratov.

FORA was rated A+ by Microfinanza in 2003. It also recently joined the Association of Russian Banks to build up its relationship with the formal domestic banking sector and attract commercial funding. FORA has since negotiated loans with several banks including Bank of Moscow, ImpEx Bank, and UralSib. One of the key constraints to borrowing from banks has been the banks' collateral requirement in the form of hard currency deposit or fixed assets. To meet this requirement, FORA engaged in negotiations with Blue Orchards in 2003 and received a $500,000 hard currency loan; this loan was pledged to local banks, which, in turn, issued ruble loans for on-lending. FORA is currently exploring the possibility of transforming into a full-fledged bank to support its continued growth strategy.

FINCA

FINCA launched its activities in Russia in 1998 under a USAID grant and currently operates through two regional offices in Samara (Volga region) and Tomsk (Siberia). FINCA Samara was established in August 1998 and has since set up offices in four additional cities. FINCA Tomsk was established in March 2001 in the framework of the Tomsk Regional Microfinance Program and has since expanded its operations to the adjacent region of Novosibirsk. FINCA Samara and FINCA Tomsk offer primarily two types of products: group loans (Business Development Group) and individual loans (Small Enterprise Loans). Business Development Group loans are issued to groups of 3–10 borrowers with loan size to each borrower ranging from $100 to 3,000 for a period of up to six months. Group loans are issued under mutual guarantee. Individual loans, which are collateralized, are generally larger and range from $500 to 17,000 for a period of up to 18 months. FINCA Samara has also been testing additional products including family loans, credit lines, and seasonal loans to meet client needs. As of end of March 2005, FINCA Samara had about 3,250 clients (the majority of whom are women) and FINCA Tomsk had about 1,330 clients (likewise, mostly women).

FINCA has been exploring various transformation options to increase its access to commercial funding. Its current plan is to establish a local joint stock company to be set up by September 2005. All assets, liabilities, and loan capital of FINCA Samara and FINCA Tomsk are expected to be merged into the new company, which will be fully owned by FINCA International Inc. and headquartered in Samara.

RWMN

Russian Women's Microfinance Network (RWMN) was established in 1998 as a non-profit partnership with the support of Women World Banking and the Ford Foundation. The objective of RWMN is to support the development of women-focused microfinance institutions throughout Russia and lend to businesswomen, mainly in the lower end of the trade business. About 70 percent of the network's clients are women and over 50 percent are single parents who lost their previous employment. The network operates in the same way as an Apex institution through five local and independent MFI partners located in Central Russia.[44] RWMN partner loans, which are extended as collateralized

---

44. Geographical coverage includes Belgorod, Kaluga, Kostroma, Tula, Tver, and Vidnoe.

individual loans, range from $100 to $10,000. As of end-2004, the network had 5,333 active clients.

In addition to a $2.3 million grant from the Ford Foundation, RWMN received grant support from the U.S. Russian Investment Fund (TUSRIF) and Citibank and a private donation from Prince Piotr Galitzine. With donor funding drying up, the network has also been exploring options to secure commercial funding and obtained loans from Raiffeisen Bank as well as Deutsche Bank and Credit Suisse microfinance investment funds. Finally, in June 2005, RWMN received the first loan extended by IFC to a Russian microfinance organization in the amount of $1 million.

RWMN was rated twice by Planet Finance and audited three times by KPMG. To further enhance its ability to attract commercial funding, the network is planning to merge its partners into one legal entity and transform into a nonbank credit organization. This change of status would make it eligible to receive deposits from legal entities but would also require a minimum charter capital of $500,000 and place the network under Central Bank supervision.

Table 5.1 Characteristics of a Selected Number of NGO MFIs (Apex)[a]

	RCCDF[b]	RWMN[c]	DID[d]	DAI[e]
Start of operations	October 1998	October 1998	March 1999	September 2001
Funding source	USAID grant for technical assistance provided by ACDI/VOCA; USDA grant for loan capital, bank loan, social investment fund loan	Grants from the Ford Foundation and TUSRIF; foreign and commercial bank loans	CIDA grant	USAID grant
Regional coverage	All of Russia	Central Russia	Southern Russia and Siberia	All of Russia
Outreach	23 regions	7 regions	4 regions	10 regions
Target clientele	First-tier and second-tier agricultural credit cooperatives (152)	Partner organizations (5)	Credit cooperatives (110)	All types of local MFIs (12)
Primary product	Loans from $21,000 to 610,000 to accredited rural cooperatives	Loans to partner organizations	Technical and financial assistance to credit union associations in 4 regions	Grants of up to $50,000 and 250,000 to eligible applicants
Interest rates:				
to intermediary	18–22% annual	19% annual	Grants	Grants
to end borrowers	24–36% annual	30–48% annual	24–48% annual	38–52% annual

(*continued*)

Table 5.1 Characteristics of a Selected Number of NGO MFIs (Apex)[a] (*Continued*)

	RCCDF[b]	RWMN[c]	DID[d]	DAI[e]
Start of operations	October 1998	October 1998	March 1999	September 2001
Loan maturity	To rural credit cooperatives: up to 12 months with pilots for up to 3 years	To partner organizations: up to 1 year	To end-borrowers (members of credit unions): up to 12 months	—
Cumulative number of loans	To rural credit cooperatives: 5,600	To end-borrowers: 36,841	To end-borrowers (members of credit unions): 62,411	22 grants
Cumulative value of loans	$36 million	To end borrowers: $44,7 million	—	Total grant amount awarded: $1,755,000
Outstanding loan amount	$8.6 million	To end-borrowers: $6,7 million	To end-borrowers (members of credit unions): $27 million	Outstanding loan portfolio of 22 grantees: $21,000,000
Number of active clients (end-borrowers)	—	5,333	56,554	NA
Average loan size to end-borrowers	$4,900	$1,200–1500 (depending on the region)	$500	—
Portfolio at risk (PAR>30 days)	5%	1.1%	2%	—
Operational self-sufficiency	213.4%	107.8%	—	—
Financial self-sufficiency	82.7%	104	—	—
Number of loans per loan officer	—	119	—	—

—. Not available.

a. These tables provide a summary of the activities of several NGO operations. Apex-type programs and direct lending operations are presented in separate tables. The information was compiled using self-reported data and/or data extracted from rating reports where available.

b. As of May 2005 (Source: ACDI/VOCA).

c. As of May 2005 (Source: RWMN).

d. As of May 2005 (Source: DID Project in Russia).

e. While DAI is a for-profit organization, since it administers a USAID grant program for microfinance organizations in Russia, it was included in this table. Data show program status as of May 2005.

Source: See table notes.

Table 5.2 Characteristics of a Selected Number of NGO MFIs (Direct Lenders)[a]

	FINCA Samara[b]	FINCA Tomsk[c]	FORA[d]	SSEDF[e]	Counterpart[f]
Start of operations	April 1998	March 2001	July 2000	September 1999	July 1998
Funding source	USAID grant (ended on October 31, 2003)	USAID grant	Grants from Opportunity International, USAID, DFID, bank loans	USAID grant for technical assistance from ACDI/VOCA and loan capital; local bank loan for loan capital	USAID grant
Regional coverage	Central Russia	Western Siberia	Western and Southern Russia	Far East	Far East
Outreach	3 regions	2 regions	21 regions	1 region	—
Target clientele	SMEs, sole proprietors, individuals	SMEs, sole proprietors	SMEs, sole proprietors	SMEs, sole proprietors	SMEs, sole proprietors
Primary product	Group loans: $100–3,000 per borrower; individual loans: $500–17,000	Group loans: $100–3,000 per borrower; individual loans: $500–17,000	Group loans up to $3,500 per borrower; individual loans up to $17,500	Group loans up to $5,000 per individual; individual loans up to $50,000	Group loans up to $10,000 per borrower; individual loans up to $30,000
Interest rates	36–42% annual	26–36% annual	36–72% annual	28–50% annual	24–48% annual
Loan maturity	Up to 18 months	Up to 18 months	Up to 24 months	Group loans up to 12 months; individual loans up to 24 months	Up to 18 months
Cumulative number of loans	27,705	15,913	102,297	6,074	3,700
Cumulative value of loans	$38,774,675	$13,972,000	$105,281,987	$11,297,790	$15,000,000
Outstanding loan amount (in million)	$5,8	$1,5	$15,3	—	—
Number of active clients	3,251	1,335	15,885	—	—
Average loan	$2,336	$880	Group loans: $1,300 per borrower; individual loans: $1,800	$1,860	$4,000

(continued)

Table 5.2 Characteristics of a Selected Number of NGO MFIs (Direct Lenders)[a] (*Continued*)

	FINCA Samara[b]	FINCA Tomsk[c]	FORA[d]	SSEDF[e]	Counterpart[f]
Start of operations	April 1998	March 2001	July 2000	September 1999	July 1998
Portfolio at risk (PAR>30 days)	1.2%	1.9%	0.28%	—	—
Operational self-sufficiency	142%	105%	127%	—	—
Financial self-sufficiency	84%	86%	97%	—	—
Number of loans per loan officer	130	89	160	54	100

—. Not available.
a. These tables provide a summary of the activities of several NGO operations. Apex-type programs and direct lending operations are presented in separate tables. The information was compiled using self-reported data and/or data extracted from rating reports where available.
b. As of March 2005 (Source: FINCA Samara).
c. As of May 2005 (Source: FINCA Tomsk).
d. As of end 2004 (Source: FORA).
e. SSEDF: Sakhalin Small Enterprise Development Foundation.
f. As of May 2005 (Source: Counterpart Enterprise Fund).
Source: See table notes.

Key Observations

■ *Pilot operations have been established across the country.* NGO operations that are predominantly donor funded cover a broad number of regions, which reflects the strategic focus of the donor community on regional development.

■ *Scale and outreach of NGO operations remain limited.* While pilot operations have been established in Siberia and the Far East, the majority remains concentrated in the Western part of the country. FORA is by far the largest NGO MFI, with about 16,000 active clients. Most other operations are small. Overall, they tend to be concentrated in urban areas of 200,000 inhabitants or more—with the exception of RCCDF, which caters to rural areas through existing rural credit cooperatives.

■ *Clients are mainly micro-entrepreneurs engaged in retail trade.* The overwhelming majority of clients are low-income micro-entrepreneurs concentrated in the retail trade sector and services with a large number of women. Manufacturing businesses represent a marginal fraction of the clientele. RCCDF is the exception, with over 90 percent of its loan capital used for agricultural production loans.

■ *Product range is mainly limited to small-scale working capital loans.* Loans are usually made as group loans under mutual guarantee or as individual loans for which collateral is required. Group loans are typically smaller than individual loans. Average loan size is below $2,000, suggesting that NGO MFIs reach a lower end of the market than does KMB Bank. Maturities and interest rates vary by region and organization but tend to range from 24 to 72 percent per annum.

■ *NGOs are looking to transform as a postdonor support strategy.* Most NGO MFIs have started to look for commercial sources of funding and are trying to develop partnerships with foreign and domestic banks. To increase their access to commercial funding, leading NGO operations are looking to transform. Interestingly, each appears to have opted for a different model, ranging from transforming into a joint stock company to a nonbank financial institution or a full-fledged bank. The more mature ones have also been rated by Microfinanza or Planet Rating and, in some instances, obtained external audits.

CHAPTER 6

Public Funds

A System of Federal and Subnational Funds

State agencies that support small business in Russia are represented by Small Business Support Funds established at the federal, regional, and/or municipal level. Services provided by these funds range from advisory and information support to direct lending and loan guarantees.

State funds typically belong to one of the three categories of a three-tier system based on Russia's territorial and administrative divisions (federal, regional, municipal). The national network of SME support funds comprises the Federal Fund, 75 regional funds, and some 200 municipal funds.[46]

While subnational funds are subject to local legislation, specific acts governing their operations must comply with the Federal Law on State Support of Small Entrepreneurship (1995), which identifies two levels of small business support funds—federal and local.

The role, functions, and rights of regional and municipal small business support funds are similar by law to those of the Federal Fund. As stipulated in the law, local funds can use state property as collateral for commercial lending to small businesses, be a shareholder in other legal entities, and finance training and scientific research. Subnational funds differ from the Federal Fund in one key aspect related to ownership structure: while the Federal Fund is 100 percent state-owned, regional and municipal funds can have mixed ownership, with up to 50 percent of shareholders composed of nonstate entities.

The impact and cost-effectiveness of public support programs are generally not tracked. Since no systematized framework of analysis allowing cross-regional comparison has been developed, information on public funds' performance remains sketchy.

---

46. See http://www.siora.ru/.

Federal Fund

The Federal Fund for Small Business Support was created in 1995 in accordance with the Law on State Support of Small Entrepreneurship. It was established as the state agency responsible for implementing the federal program for SME support and was empowered by law to perform a wide range of functions including the following:

- Facilitating a business-enabling environment and support infrastructure;
- Providing expertise in designing regional and municipal support programs and offering guidance in their implementation;
- Facilitating local and foreign investment;
- Providing advice on SME taxation and legislation issues; and
- Attracting resources for the implementation of federal and regional programs for small business support.

Though SME development is a recurrent topic of the government's economic policy, actual state support in this sector has been modest and disproportionate to the emphasis placed on the importance of SME development in public debate.

Despite its ambitious mandate imposed by law, the Federal Fund was severely underbudgeted. Its budgetary resources—which were to include federal budget allocations, proceeds from privatization of state property, and revenues from its entrepreneurial activities—varied substantially over the years. Up to 1998, a considerable part of the fund's budget originated from privatization proceeds, which became marginal after 1999. Real federal budget allocations were made only in 1996, 2000, and 2001. In 1996, its peak, the fund's budget had reached $50 million. Budgetary resources available to the fund became even scarcer in its last two years of operation as federal funds in support of small business were increasingly directed through the Ministry of Antimonopoly.

The fund used its scarce budget resources to support a wide variety of activities—providing support either directly or through seed contributions to existing intermediaries. In its early years of operation, it focused on direct lending to SMEs and provision of loan guarantees to several banks. These earlier forms of support were subsequently replaced by more indirect forms of support provided through intermediaries such as leasing companies, regional funds, and SME support agencies.[47]

The fund also reported having been involved in support of microfinance development since 2000. In 2000, in partnership with the Eurasia Foundation, the Federal Fund initiated a pilot microcredit program through regional funds in five regions (Murmansk, Novgorod, Oryol, Tula, and the Republic of Khakasiya). These funds were selected through a competitive process on the basis of their proposals for development of regional microfinance programs. The Federal Fund provided 5.5 million rubles; participating regional funds provided 6.4 million; and Eurasia contributed a $165,000 grant to cover the costs of

---

47. The Federal Fund supported and participated in the establishment of the national network of SME support funds, which comprise 75 regional and 200 municipal funds; became a shareholder in 24 regional funds and 1 municipal fund; participated in the financing of more than 100 regional programs selected on the basis of competition; and supported the development of 30 specialized SME regional leasing companies and became a shareholder in 9. It also invested directly in 17 SME support agencies and 20 informational centers (Russia FSAP data, 2003).

local capacity building in the area of microfinance and training of clients. Some 1,075 micro-loans were extended under these programs—80 percent of which were used by businesses in trade and services. Loan size was up to 100,000 rubles (about $3,000) with a maturity of up to six months.

Overall, the fund's support to microfinance was channeled through regional funds. To date, 25 regions have benefited from these programs. During 2000–2004, the Federal Fund allocated 50 million rubles to these programs, which received supplementary contributions from subnational budgets and other SME support organizations and credit institutions totaling 300 million rubles. During this period, 7,000 micro loans were reportedly issued to small businesses.

Regional and Municipal Funds

As noted above, Russia's network of state funds in support of small business includes 75 regional funds and about 200 municipal funds. At the December 2003 annual microfinance conference in St. Petersburg, it was noted that at least half of these funds had practically ceased operations owing to insufficient funding from regional and municipal budgets. The effectiveness of local funds appears to vary widely across regions. The commitment and support of regional authorities seem to be a determining factor in the funds' performance. However, to assess the specific factors responsible for these variations, a thorough case-by-case analysis would need to be conducted.

In addition to the programs implemented with the support of the Federal Fund, some regions—such as the Sverdlovsk, Voronezh, and Smolensk oblasts—have developed microfinance delivery systems based on their regional small business support fund and a network of municipal funds in rural areas. Other regional microfinance programs that have reportedly grown rapidly include Belgorod, Irkutsk, Novgorod, Ivanovo, Murmansk, and the republics of Chuvashia and Khakassia.

Government SME Support Priorities Going Forward

The Federal Fund's activities were coordinated by the Ministry of Antimonopoly's policy and entrepreneurship support, which was responsible for formulating and steering the government's SME development policy. In early 2004, the Ministry of Antimonopoly was dissolved in the wake of the overall administrative reorganization initiated by President Putin. Its functions were transferred to the Ministry of Economic Development and Trade. The government also announced the liquidation of the Federal Fund. The structure and scope of state support to SME development is thus being redefined. A 1 billion ruble guarantee provision for SME support to be administered by the Russian Development Bank was included in the 2004 State Budget, suggesting that the instrument of choice for state support to SMEs are guarantees channeled through public banks (see Box 10).

It should also be noted that, during the Sochi conference on "Access to Finance in the Southern Okrug" organized by the World Bank and the Association of Regional Banks in April 2005, representatives of the Ministry of Economic Development and Trade (MOEDT) and MOF announced that the Government of Russia was in the process of developing a guarantee support mechanism to stimulate commercial bank lending to nonbank MFIs. This mechanism was presented as an instrument designed to address the funding shortage

---

Box 10. The Russian Government's Small Business Support Guarantee Program

---

In accordance with Article 126 FZ "On the Federal Budget for 2004," the Government of Russia con-
ferred the right to grant government guarantees in support of SME development to the Russian
Development Bank (RDB). The total amount earmarked in the budget was 3 billion rubles (about
$100 million).

The Russian Development Bank. RDB was established in 1999 and is 100 percent government owned.
It was originally established to support the government investment policy by providing financial
support to priority sectors of the economy including infrastructure projects, modernization of production facilities, value-added production, and import substitution production facilities. As of
January 1, 2004, RBD was ranked 15th in equity and 26th in profits among Russian banks.

Mechanism of support to SMEs. The objective of the Guarantee Program is to broaden small business
access to finance. The procedure describing the mechanism of issuance of government guarantees
was defined by a government resolution. RBD received a 3 billion ruble sovereign guarantee backed
by the federal budget, which can be used to borrow funds on the domestic market or to grant guarantees to qualifying banks. Participating banks are to be selected by RBD based on their financial
standing and small business track record. RBD can provide loan capital to participating banks or
guarantee a portion of their outstanding small business credit portfolio (up to 70 percent). Participating banks extend loans to small businesses within preestablished lending limits. Subloans are up
to 10 million rubles for a period of up to two years. Priority is given to loans used for expansion of
manufacturing capacity, acquisition and modernization of fixed assets, and introduction of new technology. Interest rates charged to end-borrowers are set by participating banks but can be subsidized
by regional authorities using regional budgetary resources. As of mid-2004, RDB had reportedly concluded agreements with 24 partner banks.

---

experienced by non-deposit-taking MFIs and a tool to inject more liquidity into the system.
MOEDT and MOF representatives announced that the Program design would be finalized
and become effective in 2006.

Key Observations

The table presented in Appendix F, prepared by the Federal Fund, provides a list of
21 regional or municipal funds engaged in microfinance activities with Federal Fund support. The data provided by the Federal Fund reveals the following features:

- *Interest rates appear to be in line with market rates.* Interest rates vary from 1.5 to 7 percent per month. Average weighted interest rates for loans of up to 12 months is
  3.6 percent per month or about 43.2 percent on an annual basis, which appears to
  be in line with interest rates charged by other types of microfinance providers.
  While there is no automatic correlation, overall interest rates appear to be higher
  in the Eastern part of Russia than in Western and Central areas.
- *Outreach is limited.* The vast majority of beneficiaries are small entrepreneurs involved
  in trade and services. The number of borrowers ranges from a handful to 6,600.
- *Loan sizes are relatively small,* ranging from $100 to 1,000, which is less than micro-
  finance loans offered by most NGOs and KMB Bank, suggesting that these funds
  cater to the low end of the microfinance market.
- *Loan maturity is short,* ranging from 10 days to a year, with the majority of funds
  offering loans of up to six months.

CHAPTER 7

Overall Trends in Russian Microfinance

*T*he microfinance industry has largely developed as a result of donor initiative and financial support. Compared to other regions of the world, the microfinance industry in Central and Eastern Europe can still be classified as young. Microfinance institutions in Europe and Central Asia (excluding credit cooperatives) have been operating for an average of five years compared to an average of nine years for MFIs on a global basis (MIX 2005; see Appendix J for more details). As in other European and Central Asian countries, Russia's microfinance providers have relied on donor assistance for their development. EBRD has played a prominent role since 1994 through its Russia Small Business Fund (RSBF) program. In addition, USAID has played an important role in establishing the Russian Microfinance Center and initiating several NGO programs. The U.S. Government is also providing assistance to the rural credit cooperative sector through ACDI/VOCA.

Some of the key donors are scaling back their assistance to microfinance. Although EBRD will be continuing its support to RSBF until 2010, the other major donor—USAID—is beginning to scale back its involvement in the microfinance sector. The Russian Microfinance Center (RMC) was created in 2002 as a noncommercial foundation as part of the USAID-sponsored Russia Microfinance Sector Support Program. The RMC has played an instrumental advocacy role for the development of microfinance in Russia. To diversify its funding sources and ensure that it can continue operating beyond USAID's withdrawal, the RMC is planning to establish a revolving loan fund, which will operate as an Apex and provide funding on a commercial basis to local MFIs.

All four main types of institutional providers are present in the region. These are commercial banks (downscaling and greenfield), NGO MFIs, membership-based institutions such as rural cooperatives and credit unions, and public funds. However, despite its vast size, Russia has fewer microfinance providers compared to some of the smaller countries in the region even though potential demand from the micro and small business sector is estimated to be in the multibillion-dollar range.

With the exception of KMB Bank, commercial banks are not dominant players in providing microfinance services. The first commercial bank downscaling experience in the region was Sberbank (with EBRD support). KMB Bank was established in 1999 by EBRD and has since played a leading role in microlending through its expanding regional network. Although KMB Bank's performance has provided evidence that microfinance banking can work in Russia with introduction of appropriate technology, the vast majority of banks have not engaged in microlending. At the same time, while small business lending continues to be perceived as high risk, there has been significant growth in consumer lending over the past couple of years—a portion of which may actually reflect an increase in small business lending and a beginning trend toward market-driven (versus donor-driven) downscaling. In addition, VTB, Russia's second-largest state bank recently launched a large-scale micro and small business lending program.

Some of the dominant NGO MFIs in the sector are initiating strategies to transform into formal sector institutions. FINCA Samara and RWMN are in the process of transforming from noncommercial organizations into formal sector institutions. Both have operated under an ambiguous legal and regulatory environment for NGO MFIs and have decided for strategic reasons to seek other institutional options to continue expanding their client base and attract additional funding sources to scale up their operations. RWMN is seeking to transform into a nonbank credit organization, which would allow it to collect deposits from legal entities while placing the network under Central Bank supervision. FINCA Samara is planning to transform into a joint stock company. Finally, FORA, by far the largest NGO MFI, is in the process of transforming into a full-fledged bank.

Links between NGO MFIs and the banking sector have been emerging. Although the links between NGO MFIs and the banking sector are in early stages of development, there are a few examples of bank-NGO cooperation. FORA has joined the Association of Russian Banks and initiated a relationship with the domestic banking sector to explore the possibility of raising commercial funding for its expansion. Both FORA and RWMN use foreign currency loans as guarantees to cover ruble credit lines received from local banks for on-lending to their clients.

There has been a rapid expansion in the number of member-based organizations. In the last five years, there has been an accelerated growth in the number of agricultural credit cooperatives and citizens' cooperatives, whose membership totals about 420,800 today compared to some 33,200 in 1998. The membership per institution remains low and is capped at 2,000 by law. This rapid growth has occurred despite a fragmented legal and regulatory framework and limited access to funding sources. In light of the limited penetration of the banking sector and the inability of NGO MFIs to offer savings products, these institutions fulfill an important role in providing financial services to their members. In underbanked rural areas, rural credit cooperatives are often the only channel for small farmers and non-agricultural SMEs to access credit.

Microfinance providers are exploring the possibility of expanding their product range. Key providers are seeking to scale up their operations and keep up with the competition by broadening their product line. For example, facing increased competition from banks in the area of consumer lending, some credit cooperatives have been seeking to expand their small business lending portfolio and develop new products such as mortgage loans.

CHAPTER 8

Key Challenges Going Forward and Recommendations

While microfinance providers have enjoyed significant growth over the past three to five years, microfinance in Russia is still at an early stage of development. Potential demand for services also appears to far outweigh the supply—suggesting that microfinance has a vast upside potential.

As described above, microfinance is provided by a wide range of retail financial and nonfinancial institutions ranging from banks to specialized credit-only MFIs and credit cooperatives. These institutions, which serve various segments of the small market niche are at different stages of development. Some, which have benefited from early donor support and developed in economically more prosperous regions, have enjoyed steady growth and are operating on a quasi- or full cost recovery basis. Others, which are in their formative stages of development, are still small and are yet to pass the sustainability threshold.

On the issue of sustainability, it should be noted that while financial sustainability is essential to reach scale and ensure continuity in the provision of financial services, some microfinance lenders may never become sustainable. As any enterprise, microfinance lenders are subject to a variety of internal and external factors that can impact their operations and restrict their chances to reach sustainability. These factors may include lack of professional skills, poor governance, unfavorable market conditions, and/or unfavorable local operating, legal, and political environment.

In addition, some microfinance operations set up in economically depressed or post-conflict areas may be developed from the onset with a strict poverty alleviation focus that precludes profitability.

For mature retail providers to continue their expansion and reach a larger number of clients and for new or young providers to develop in a sustainable manner and deepen their outreach, a number of conditions will need to be in place:

(1) *At the policy level,* policymakers will need to foster a conducive environment that recognizes microfinance as an integral part of the country's financial system and promotes the development of a wide range of financial service providers while protecting consumers (depositors, savers, and borrowers).

(2) *At the infrastructure level,* it will be important to strengthen microfinance providers' networks and associations, which play an instrumental advocacy role, facilitate information exchange, promote use of standardized performance reporting, and provide business development services and specialized training to the sector.

(3) *At the retail level,* since donors are expected to scale back, MFIs will need to explore new sources of funding to support their continued growth and development beyond donor funding. To reach scale and streamline their delivery cost, MFIs will also need to explore different partnership options with commercial banks and/or among themselves.

The specific recommendations presented below are based on these three dimensions. It should be noted that these recommendations, which are not meant to be exhaustive, are based on the findings of this study and echo a number of recommendations formulated in prior research, notably Foster, Greene, and Pytkowska in *Study of the State of Microfinance in the CEE and the NIS* (2003) supported by CGAP, which provides an interesting "framework for action." They also draw on the discussions of the Access to Finance conference organized by the World Bank in Sochi in April 2005.

Recommendations for Policymakers

▨ *Maintain a conducive enabling environment.* The sustainable development of microfinance will depend on a number of general conditions under the control of policymakers. These conditions include maintaining a stable macroeconomic and banking sector environment, improving the business climate through further deregulation and elimination of red tape, introducing International Accounting Standards, strengthening the lending environment and infrastructure by facilitating the establishment of credit bureaus, improving collateral foreclosure procedures, and simplifying statutory requirements for small business lending.

▨ *Provide a clear and conducive legal framework for credit cooperatives and eliminate undue restrictions.* The development of credit cooperatives in Russia has been impeded by the slow development of enabling legislation. In the absence of a clear federal legal framework, some regions, such as the Volgograd region, adopted local legislation to supplement the existing legal vacuum and recognized credit cooperatives as a special type of lending institution. The Federal Law on Rural Credit Cooperatives adopted in 1995 and the Law on Credit Consumer Cooperatives of Citizens adopted in 2001 have since facilitated the development of the credit cooperative sector on a larger scale. However, the current laws contain a number of restrictions that may hamper the continued development of the sector in the medium term. These include the maximum membership cap (2,000), limits on the membership of nonagricultural producers in rural cooperatives, and the cap on the share of business loans in citizens' cooperatives' credit portfolios (50 percent). A new framework law on credit cooperatives, which would lift several of the above restrictions, has been pending in the Duma since 2002. While the adoption of this framework law on credit cooperatives may be beneficial to the credit cooperative sector as a whole, it will be important to ensure that the final draft does not undo some of the key provisions included in the current laws in force, including the authorization for credit cooperatives to form multitier organizations.

- *Develop a clear supervisory framework for all MFIs—and credit cooperatives in particular.* The aim of a supportive regulatory framework is to build strong regulated and unregulated institutions of all types to provide services on a sustainable basis under shared performance standards. This involves defining tiers of financial institutions with different degrees of regulatory requirements. As the primary purpose of regulation is to protect depositors, regulating authorities should concentrate on deposit-taking organizations. NGO MFIs in Russia, which do not take deposits, are rightfully exempt from supervision. Those that are seeking to transform into nonbank credit organizations as well as microfinance banks are already or will become subject to CBR supervision. As for credit cooperatives, they are currently unsupervised. Since credit cooperatives have expanded rapidly over the past three to five years and are likely to absorb a growing volume of member savings, government authorities will need to develop an appropriate framework for their supervision. As their first priority, policymakers will need to assign responsibility for regulating the cooperative sector to a clear and adequately equipped government entity. Second, they will need to determine which model of supervision to adopt and evaluate the current capacity of supervisory authorities as well as the potential for industry self-regulation.

- *Analyze the performance of state funds in delivering credit.* There is a lack of information on the performance of public funds. To assess their effectiveness, the government should collect information on repayment rates, loan collection efficiency, incidence of loan defaults, adequacy of loan loss provisions and claims on budgetary or fiscal resources for loan guarantees. This would help rationalize the role of government as a direct provider of financial services.

- *Provide targeted support.* International experience suggests that governments are not good at providing financial services directly. International practice also tends to frown upon subsidized lending. However, policymakers may consider providing targeted support to promote the development of existing microfinance providers through capacity building and, if warranted, possibly through the use of carefully designed credit lines or guarantee support mechanisms. Policymakers at the regional level should also facilitate the scaling up and replication of models and institutions such as rural credit cooperatives and credit unions, which have proved that they can work well in pilot regions.

- *Improve micro and small enterprise data collection.* Recent empirical studies have suggested that the small enterprise sector plays a much larger role in the Russian economy than is captured by statistics. To obtain a more accurate estimate of the profile and share of micro and small business in the Russian economy, the Government of

Russia should improve its data collection, which would in turn help fine-tune public support programs designed to stimulate small business growth.

Recommendations for Retail Providers

▦ *As donor funding declines, MFIs will need to explore alternative sources of financing.* USAID, which has been a key player in facilitating the incubation of the sector, will close its financial sector support program in 2007. Commercial funding is expected to replace donor funding over time. Commercial funding includes quasi-commercial sources such as the International Finance Corporation (IFC), commercial banks, commercial investment funds, and socially motivated or ethical investment funds.[48] MFIs should familiarize themselves and keep current on the growing available supply of such funds as well as domestic funding opportunities, notably through the banks.

▦ *To strengthen their capital-raising capabilities, MFIs will need to further improve their performance and transparency.* MFIs' difficulties to attract commercial funding lie in commercial funders' perception that microfinance is a high-risk activity, driven by social returns rather than the commercial bottom line, and in the funders' inability to provide adequate collateral (notably fixed assets). For MFIs to demonstrate their creditworthiness and commercial value as investment options, they must strengthen their financial performance and transparency of financial reporting. The following actions (some of which have already been undertaken by leading NGO MFIs) can help strengthen MFIs' transparency and increase their capital raising capabilities:

   ✔ Undergo a professional rating by a qualified international microfinance rating agency.[49]

   ✔ Report to the MIX Bulletin, which uses standardized financial ratios and provides reliable comparative performance data and benchmarks by type of institution, region, and number of years in operation.

   ✔ Obtain an annual external financial audit based on International Accounting Standards.[50]

▦ *To sustain competition and adapt to changing demand, MFIs will need to increase their product range.* Until recently, most MFIs focused on building their capacity around simple credit-only products for which demand has far outweighed supply. However, as they mature, MFIs will likely face increased competitive pressures to diversify and innovate. These pressures may come from increased competition among existing providers and commercial banks. NGO MFIs and urban-based credit cooperatives report that they are already facing steep competition from commercial banks in the area of consumer lending. Competitive pressures may also result

---

48. A list of commercial providers is attached in Appendix H.

49. To enhance financial accountability and transparency, the Inter-American Development Bank and CGAP launched the "Microfinance Rating and Assessment Fund" in 2001. The fund was designed to cofinance the cost of rating MFIs. There are six qualified international ratings agencies under the program: ACCION International, M-CRIL of India, Microfinanza of Italy, Micro Rate, PlaNet Finance, and WOCCU (World Bank 2003).

50. This option may only be feasible for larger, well-established MFIs given its cost.

from structural changes in the economy. As the economy grows, an important fraction of the traditional clientele of microfinance providers (market vendors, small kiosks) is likely to be crowded out by emerging mid-size firms capable of offering a broader range of products at lower prices. Finally, as the economy develops and employment opportunities increase, some of the small entrepreneurs, who turned to small business out of necessity, may give up their self-employment status for a permanent position.[51] As competition for clients increases and a shift in clientele takes place, MFIs will need to increase their outreach and develop new products:

- ✔ MFIs should prepare for the next generation of microfinance services. With the exception of downscaling and greenfield banks, microfinance providers are prohibited from taking deposits. In the short run, product innovation is thus likely to be in credit-based products. Demand for new products such as longer-term investment loans, microleasing, and housing loans is likely to be high.

- ✔ With respect to credit unions, generally speaking, the credit technology employed by credit unions is well-suited to consumer lending. Loans are typically granted as a multiple of accumulated savings, and most of the loans granted by credit unions are used for consumption purposes. Thus, if credit unions are also to become significant suppliers of finance to small and micro-enterprises, they will require significant institutional strengthening and capacity building in the areas of credit methodology, product development, and information technology.

■ *To reach scale, MFIs will need to explore various partnership options.* Russian MFIs have very small-scale operations. While they may enjoy higher portfolio growth as they mature, non-deposit-taking MFIs will lack sufficient resources to scale up in any significant way. Their outreach will thus likely remain limited unless they develop strategic partnership alliances. MFIs and commercial banks could develop complementary and mutually beneficial relationships. Commercial banks could tap into the microfinance market without incurring additional infrastructure and technology cost by providing wholesale funds to MFIs. Other forms of partnerships may include sharing facilities, cross-selling each other's services, and client referral (MFIs referring creditworthy clients to banks and banks referring nonbankable clients to MFIs). However, as international experience shows, the fastest and most cost-effective way of reaching scale may be the commercial bank downscaling model where microfinance services are channeled through existing bank networks and retail branches:

- ✔ NGO MFIs and credit cooperatives should explore partnerships and alliances with commercial banks.

- ✔ Russian banks interested in exploring downscaling models should review international downscaling experience and familiarize themselves with specialized lending technology developed by institutions such as ShoreBank and IPC to reach low-income clients.

---

51. Job growth in firms with fewer than 30 employees grew more slowly than those with 30–100 employees. According to the World Bank's Country Economic Memorandum for the Russian Federation (2004), the rapid job growth in small firms compared to micro-enterprises between 1999 and 2002 is consistent with a "maturing" of the SME sector. Many of those micro-firms have now grown into small firms, and new entry and growth at the micro level may have slowed.

▪ *MFIs committed to the low end of the market should explore new delivery methods.* Providing financial services to the poor tends to be more expensive than serving the middle to upper end of the microfinance market because of the difficulties in achieving economies of scale. Experience shows that, as a rule, credit cooperatives and NGO MFIs have demonstrated a greater ability to reach the poor (including low-income rural communities) than have microfinance or downscaling banks. This may be the result of both an explicit organizational commitment to serve the poor and competitive pressure from banks, which capture the higher end of the market. Interestingly, contrary to the assumption that MFIs move up market as they mature, the study of microfinance in Central and Eastern Europe and CIS reveals that some mature MFIs have deepened their poverty outreach since their establishment. Expanding outreach to the underserved can be done through staff incentives, new product development, and innovative delivery channels. Some MFIs have successfully developed and continue to experiment with methods of delivering services to the poor cost-effectively. To increase their rural outreach, MFIs will also need to develop tailored products taking into account the seasonal nature of cash flows in the agricultural sector.

✔ MFIs interested in deepening their outreach would benefit from reviewing existing experiences and familiarizing themselves with the vast body of knowledge and information on outreach and product development accumulated by CGAP, MicroSave, and the Poland-based Microfinance Center.

APPENDIXES

Microfinance Demand Estimates

FINCA-SME Resource Center Microfinance Study

The analysis conducted by FINCA and the SME Resource Center in 2003 evaluated the demand for microloans based on an empirical analysis of a cross section of (1) enterprises with fewer than 10 employees and (2) unemployed individuals potentially interested in initiating small business activities.

(1) *Small enterprises* in Russia fall into one of three categories—small businesses registered as legal entities, sole proprietors registered as individuals, and individual farms. The demand study estimated potential demand from the lower segment of each category by isolating those with fewer than 10 employees.

(2) To assess potential demand from *unemployed individuals,* the study used and applied selected characteristics observed among active entrepreneurs (including gender profile, age, education level, and prior employment status and position) to identify those with entrepreneurial potential and thus likely to engage in business activities.

Based on these calculations, the study concluded that there is potential demand for microfinance from about *2 million micro-enterprises* (80 percent of which are sole proprietors) and about *188,000 unemployed individuals* believed to have entrepreneurial potential. These data do not include potential additional significant demand from employed individuals who may want to initiate business activities to supplement their incomes or from individuals who may want to borrow small amounts for personal and consumer purposes (such as health or housing repair).

To translate the potential demand in monetary terms, the number of potential clients in each category was further multiplied by the average expected loan size. The potential demand on the part of existing small businesses alone was estimated in the Rub 233–581.5 billion range ($7.7–19.4 billion).

The study estimated that the volume of supply of microcredits amounted to about $52 million at the time and thus concluded that microfinance providers cover less than 1 percent of the potential market.

Demand Estimate for Cooperative Credit in Rural Areas

In a recent study prepared under a United Nations Development Programme (UNDP)–funded project (Cordonnier 2004), demand for cooperative finance in rural areas was estimated on the basis of current and projected demand from household plots and private farmers. The study outlined three scenarios (high, medium, low) based on the assumption of a stable GDP growth of 5 percent a year, a stable share of agriculture in GDP of 7 percent, and available liquid collateral (animal stock) that could be pledged by borrowers to guarantee their credits. Results showed that the total amount of potential demand for credit varied from $1.13–3.28 billion for 2004 and $1.59–4.4 billion for 2010. In dollar amount per rural inhabitant, the demand was estimated to range from about $29–84 in 2004 and $41–113 in 2010 (see Table A.1).

Table A.1 Demand Estimates for Cooperative Finance in Rural Areas						
	High scenario		Medium scenario		Low scenario	
	Total amount ($ billion)	Amount per rural inhabitant ($)	Total amount ($ billion)	Amount per rural inhabitant ($)	Total amount ($ billion)	Amount per rural inhabitant ($)
2004	3.28	84.2	2.21	56.6	1.13	29
2010	4.4	112.8	3	76.8	1.59	40.8

Source: Adapted by the author from *Development of a National System of Rural Cooperative Banking in Russia: Some Proposals Based on International Experience,* Dr. Christopher Cordonnier, Head of Research, UNDP's Russian Farm Entrepreneurs Development Program, March 2004.

As rural credit cooperatives currently provide only $0.6 of cooperative credit per rural inhabitant, the study revealed a significant gap in financing and a vast untapped market.

Greenfield and Downscaling Experiences in Eastern Europe and the CIS

ProCredit Bank, Bulgaria

ProCredit Bank (formerly known as the Microfinance Bank of Bulgaria) was established by EBRD, IFC, IMI, and DEG in 2001 to provide financial services to micro and small enterprises. The bank's target group comprises micro, small, and medium-sized companies in trade, production, and services. In addition to providing loans, the bank provides a full range of financial services to its target group including current accounts services; deposit and savings facilities; leasing; currency exchange operations; bank cards; e-banking; international operations, including documentary collection; letters of credit; and bank guarantees. In 2003, it also introduced a housing loan product and has disbursed over 2,000 housing loans to date. ProCredit Bank began operating in Sofia and has since expanded its operations to cover all major regions of the country, with 28 branches serving a total of 28,000 clients. Further regional expansion is planned for 2004–2008 with the opening of an additional 10 branches foreseen in 2004. Since start of operations, the bank has provided loans to Bulgarian micro and small enterprises totaling €144 million. ProCredit Bank's financial position has also been improving significantly over the past three years. Its return on assets increased from 7 percent in 2001 to 13 percent in 2003, and net profit grew to EUR 1.2 million while its operational cost decreased.

Downscaling—The Kazakhstan Small Business Program (KSBP)

KSBP was established in April 1998 by EBRD to provide finance to small businesses through participating downscaling commercial banks and increase their credit capabilities. EBRD contributed $175 million in credit facility, which was matched by a $25 million contribution by IFC while Technical Assistance for the CIS (TACIS) and other donors funded the technical assistance package aimed at developing partner banks' skills.

KSBP is working with seven commercial banks including the largest local banks. By February 2004 all urban centers in Kazakhstan were covered by the program. Partner banks have opened small business lending units in 135 branches and an additional 50 outlets in 39 cities (some as small as 20,000 inhabitants). The program's outstanding portfolio is currently over $162 million, with about 43,000 loans outstanding. KSBP targets small enterprises (employing fewer than 100 people) in all sectors of the economy; 90 percent of these have never had access to bank loans before. Loan amounts range from $100 to 200,000 and monthly interest rates vary between 2 and 2.9 percent on Kazakh Tenge–denominated loans and between 1.3 and 2 percent on U.S. dollar loans. Eighty-five percent of the loans are under $5,000 and over 50 percent of the newly disbursed loans are express microloans—a newly developed product for very small customers needing uncollateralized working capital loans that can be disbursed instantly.

There are currently 535 loan officers working in the micro and small enterprise departments of the partner banks, disbursing about 4,000 micro and small loans per month. Arrears are low (arrears over 30 days stood at 0.25 percent of the outstanding portfolio in February 2004). A newly developed profit center accounting method, which is being tested, is yielding strong evidence that the micro and small enterprise business has passed the profitability threshold and is as or more profitable than the average Kazakh bank. Partner banks have committed their own funds to the program (over 40 percent of the portfolio is now being financed with the banks' own funds) and are investing continuously in the training of new loan officers and the opening of micro and small enterprise departments and outlets in new localities.

The Brazilian
Microfinance Experience

Extracts from "Brazil—Access to Financial Services,"
World Bank Report No. 27773-BR, February 2004

*A**ctive involvement of the Brazilian Government:* There was a remarkable recent acceleration in the development of the Brazilian microfinance sector in the late 1990s. This accelerated growth can be attributed to a series of factors including new political paradigms leading to a series of legal and regulatory changes favoring the expansion of the sector, a major new large scale microcredit experiment—the 'CrediAmigo' program through BNB (a state-owned development bank) and active government financial backing to emerging microfinance institutions through credit offered by the Brazilian state-owned development bank BNDES.

The recent expansion of microfinance has been largely government led and channeled through the substantial presence of two public banks—BNB and BNDES. Microfinance institutions have also relied substantially on relatively low cost government lines of credit extended at below comparable market rates. Recent changes introduced by the government include microfinance operations destined for low income earners and small businesses to be funded by a minimum 2 percent of the financial institution's sight deposits. The new measures create the possibility of additional reserve requirements for banks which do not participate in certain programs of access.

The Brazilian credit cooperative system has also made important advances, particularly since the mid-1990s, with the permission to establish cooperative banks. These have allowed for rapid expansion of credit cooperatives combined with growing professionalism in cooperative management, information, accounting, staff training and incentives, and internally administered prudential standards. New measures introduced in 2003 have further favored the expansion of cooperatives, expanding membership in remote areas by allowing 'open admission' credit cooperatives to be established, and by creating a more level playing field with banks through the harmonization of capital requirements.

Credi Amigo—a Downscaling Program which Became a Major Player in Microfinance

In 1997, enthused by its new management and by the new attention to microfinance in political spheres within Brazil, Banco do Nordeste do Brasil (BNB), a state-owned development bank with a mandate to promote economic development in the northeastern states, launched a large scale microfinance program, which has remained unrivalled in scale in Brazil. At end 2001, it served nearly 60 percent of MFI client micro-entrepreneurs and held about 45 percent of their outstanding loans.

The program, known as CrediAmigo, benefited from the technical advice of ACCION International (a group with strong experience in solidarity group lending) as well as from the CGAP (Consultative Group to Assist the Poorest), and was financially supported by the World Bank. CrediAmigo was committed to incorporate best-practice principles emerging from successful microfinance institutions in the world. These included (i) solidarity group lending; (ii) targeting the informal sector; (iii) charging interest rates high enough to provide a return on assets sufficient to permit financial sustainability; (iv) starting with small loan amounts and gradually escalating loan size with repeat loans; (v) amortizing loans regularly; (vi) offering incentives for regular repayment through discounts on the last installment, and penalizing borrowers if repayment falls behind schedule. The program also adopted the principles of product differentiation (separating its identity from BNB through a separate entrance or premises, for each branch office. Unlike some successful microfinance programs in other countries, there are no obligatory savings requirements (microfinance entities in Brazil cannot accept deposits).

CrediAmigo adopts additional good practices to safeguard its portfolio. A potential client microenterprise must be at least a year old with demonstrated cash flow potential. Its solidarity group members must know each other well but relatives are excluded. Each group elects a representative and adopts a name. Newly formed solidarity group[s] undergo training by loan officers on group liability and loan characteristics. Initially, loans were exclusively for working capital purposes. Later, individual loans were introduced based on client records of at least two solidarity group loans. And by offering life insurance policies to its borrowers during the term of its loans, CrediAmigo protects itself from eventual death of borrowers.

Portfolio growth: CrediAmigo's minimum loan sizes, for first time loans, have ranged from around R$200 to R$700 and each subsequent loan may be 50 percent larger than the previous loan. Its average loan size in December 2002 was only R$605, confirming a focus on the poor. Female participation, however, corresponds to the population average, at 48 percent. Loan terms range from three to six months for solidarity group loans. Interest rates are higher than public bank enterprise loans but lower than consumer credit or even rates charged by some nonbanks such as factoring companies. The program began with a 5 percent flat monthly rate, which has since been reduced to 3.5 percent. Initially, there was a high loan renewal rate, of about 85 percent, and an increasing number of new clients per loan officer. Time between application and disbursement for first time borrowers is seven days, while for repeated borrowers it is 24 hours.

Links to BNB: CrediAmigo represents less than one percent of loan assets of BNB, and is being managed as an independent profit center with the goal of monitoring progress towards self-sustainability and eventual separation from BNB. As part of BNB, CrediAmigo is supervised by the Central Bank. To date, it has received its funds on a 100 percent basis from BNB, which are indexed to the CDI rate, which closely tracks the Selic or interbank rate. However, if CrediAmigo had to raise funds from deposits (and comply with reserve requirements) or borrow at market rates from commercial banks or through the issue of its own paper, its funding costs may rise. In terms of operating costs, the program has made every effort to separate its costs from those of BNB and also to prorate the use of BNB resources. Such a separation is however partially dependent on the capacity of BNB for monitoring cost centers. Critically, CrediAmigo has kept costs down and enhanced client focus by separating its labor and staff from the BNB. Its image differentiation in terms of its branches has also relieved it from obligations of complying with costly bank branch opening requirements.

Portfolio Quality and Financial Performance: CrediAmigo initiated operations in 5 BNB branches in November 1997, and expanded in five months to 50 additional branches, but with ensuing poor portfolio quality. With a renewed commitment to focus on portfolio quality and productivity, CrediAmigo was able to achieve a more stable and sustainable rate of growth. Today, CrediAmigo distributes its products through 164 of Banco do Nordeste's 174 branches. By May 2003, CrediAmigo was among the largest microfinance institutions in Latin America, with 123,000 clients and an active portfolio of R$72 million.

Delinquency rates at CrediAmigo were initially uneven. Delinquency rose sharply in the first year following the surge of expansion, but management reacted promptly by writing off bad loans and in early 1999, by modifying its performance-based incentive scheme for staff. It also installed a detailed portfolio monitoring system for delinquency at the loan officer level. Since its inception, CrediAmigo has been aware of the needs to monitor and control costs and to operate on the basis of profit centers. Today, each branch is a profit center. Today its portfolio quality and staff productivity compare favorably with international good practice. Only 4 percent of its loans were overdue, using a strict 30-day portfolio-at-risk measure, in accordance with Central Bank requirements. Its annualized loan loss rate is 2.7 percent, after fully provisioning all loans with payment 360 days or more overdue. As to productivity, loan officers with nine months or more of experience are each handling an average of 313 clients. Salary expenses as a percentage of loan portfolio decreased from 139 percent in December 1998 to 27 percent in May 2001.

In terms of profitability, CrediAmigo has progressed positively. About 145 of CrediAmigo's 164 branches are operationally sustainable. Since June 2000, CrediAmigo has presented positive returns on average assets but in 2002, profits dropped. Learning to maintain good portfolio quality is one of the key challenges which CrediAmigo faces in controlling operating expenses, which remained high at 37 percent of total assets, as of December 2002.

Implications for Brazil's Microfinance Sector: The story of CrediAmigo clearly dominates Brazil's microfinance sector. It has clearly demonstrated the existence of a market niche for microfinance and has also demonstrated the means for its achievement. It incorporates many examples of recognized good practice in microfinance lending techniques. It also shows that rapid growth must be tempered with an eye on quality and that learning the microfinance culture takes time.

To what extent does its story provide commercial banks with a model for 'downscaling'? CrediAmigo demonstrates that, under appropriate conditions and following specific practices, a "downscaling" strategy for commercial banks (i.e., targeting lower income individuals or smaller businesses) could be viable. CrediAmigo also suggests that an existing branch network can greatly help the rollout of microfinance products. Alternatively, partnerships allowing microfinance specialists to distribute their products via bank networks could also be successful strategies to develop large-scale microfinance services.

The Polish Credit Union Experience[52]

In 1989, the Solidarity Party of Poland approached the World Council of Credit Unions (WOCCU) to conduct a feasibility study on how to revive the Polish credit union movement. Initially, the U.S. credit union movement had donated seed capital to promote education on how to set up and run a credit union and to create the required legal framework for the redevelopment of the industry in the post-Soviet era. In 1992, the Polish Credit Union system was initiated with the support of technical assistance provided by WOCCU and funded by USAID. In 1993, USAID launched a much larger project—"Building the Polish Savings and Credit Union System"—which was extended twice and shifted its focus from institution building in its early incarnation to strengthening of the system in later years.

The Polish Credit Union system consists of the following subsidiary or affiliated organizations: Credit unions, the National Association of Cooperative Savings and Credit Unions (NACSCU), the Credit Union Mutual Insurance Society, the Credit Union Life Insurance Society, Asekuracjia Insurance Brokerage Co., the Credit Union Investment Fund Society, the Credit Union Financial Society, the H&S Software Co., the Foundation for Polish Credit Unions, the Higher School for Administration and Finance, the Society for Promotion of Financial Education, the Credit Union Publishing House, and the Credit Union Arbitration.

Credit unions in Poland offer a sophisticated variety of products and services: personal accounts, term deposits, savings accounts, short-term instant loans, long- and medium-term credits, long-term housing loans, business services accounts, credit and money transfers, credit and debit cards, ATM services, electronic payments of monthly bills, payment settlements, insurance services, and pension funds products.

---

52. Proceedings of the 7th Annual Conference of the Microfinance Institutions in C&EE and the NIS, 27–29 May 2004, Warsaw, Poland.

NACSCU is the Apex organization through which all credit unions are authorized to operate in Poland. NACSCU has been vested with the responsibility of establishing prudential standards and norms for credit unions and of enforcing these norms through auditing and supervision. To effectively monitor the compliance of these standards, NACSCU requires strict monthly reporting by all credit unions.

The Credit Union Mutual Insurance Society provides credit unions and their members with a variety of important insurance products such as deposit insurance coverage, property and casualty insurance, credit disability insurance, and fidelity bonding insurance. The Credit Union Life Insurance Society, on the other hand, provides life insurance products to credit union members such as credit life insurance, life savings insurance, funeral insurance, and individual life insurance. Asekuracjia Insurance Brokerage Co. offers insurance brokerage services and provides credit services to credit union members via credit agents.

The Credit Union Investment Fund Society invests the savings of members through funds into financial instruments available on the market. It also designs and manages investment funds products. The Credit Union Financial Society provides long-term housing loans and financing through leasing to credit union members.

The H&S Software Company has been the exclusive provider of software programs to all credit unions since 1992. H&S also handles the purchase of office supplies, as well as equipment and furniture for credit unions.

The Foundation for Polish Credit Unions supports the development of the credit union movement through promotion of credit unions and financial cooperatives principles, as well as training and education. It also provides technical and financial assistance to other credit unions in the region (Ukraine, Lithuania, Latvia, Romania, and Bulgaria).

The Higher School for Administration and Finance offers graduate and postgraduate courses in business administration and finance to credit union executives and staff as well as specialized training courses geared toward the specific needs of credit unions. The Society for Promotion of Financial Education, on the other hand, is responsible for promoting financial education to individual members and provides legal and financial assistance, including debt counseling to individuals.

The Credit Union Publishing House produces publications promoting credit unions and their philosophy. It also publishes "Money and Bond," a quarterly that promotes economic education and understanding of sound business and financial management practices.

The Credit Union Arbitration settles extrajudicial disputes between credit unions and their members.

Over its past 12 years of existence, the Polish Credit Union system has expanded its outreach rapidly and, to date, unites over 1 million members. Total assets have increased from an initial Zl 4 million to 3.5 billion.

The Polish credit union movement is considered one of the most successful cases in Eastern Europe and the former Soviet Union. Its success is attributed to a combination of factors: the Solidarity Party was highly supportive of credit unions' development and openly encouraged its members to either form a new credit union or join existing ones; many people were predisposed to joining and forming credit unions because of the overwhelming support of the Solidarity Party; and the favorable macroeconomic and hospitable regulatory environment together with dedicated, vigorous local management teams contributed significantly to the overall success of the industry.

Description of Specialized Russian NGO MFI Programs

Development Alternatives Inc.

In 2001, Development Alternatives, Inc. (DAI) was awarded a USAID-funded Microfinance Support Project consisting of two components: establishing and supporting the Russian Microfinance Center (RMC) and running a grant program to support local MFIs.

RMC was established in the summer of 2002 as a noncommercial organization to support the development of the microfinance industry in Russia. It has since become a primary information clearinghouse and a specialized training and consulting center for local MFIs, and has emerged as an industry lobbyist advocating for policy, legal, and regulatory changes and promoting industry standards.[53]

The Targeted Awards-Innovation Support Program (TAISP) was initially designed to provide grants to Russian nonbank microfinance organizations that had not received any donor funding during the previous five years. Grants could be used for loan capital, operating cost, fixed assets, expansion, product innovation, or to cover the cost of training and outside services (audits). By December 2003, 84 applications had been received, 54 of which did not meet the eligibility criteria. As of March 2005, 22 grants had been awarded totaling $1,755,000.

In the summer of 2003, DAI and the RMC together with USAID revisited the original grant concept and opted for an alternative approach. In 2003, a feasibility study was launched to explore the possibility of setting up a Revolving Microfinance Fund, which would lend

---

53. RMC set up a working group, which developed a Glossary of Standard Financial Terms and Ratios based on CGAP financial standards. RMC also organizes annual microfinance conferences, which bring together local practitioners, policymakers, and international experts to exchange information and discuss industry developments. Finally, RMC provides training in a variety of topics ranging from basic microfinance to liquidity and delinquency management, financial analysis, and interest rate setting.

resources on a commercial basis to a wider range of microfinance organizations for on-lending to micro-enterprise clients. The proposal was reviewed and approved by USAID.

The RMC loan fund will be incorporated as a for-profit company, initially owned by the RMC with the participation of minority shareholders such as the Association of Russian Banks. The fund will make loans to microfinance organizations of different types secured by a whole or partial assignment of their loan portfolios. Loans will be made in rubles. The majority of the loan capital will be contributed by USAID through a grant either to the RMC or to the loan fund directly. The fund's initial capital will be about $2 million. Dividends received from the fund by the RMC are also expected to contribute to the continuation of RMC's operations after USAID's withdrawal. The fund is currently being registered and its launch date is scheduled for the third quarter of 2005.

Counterpart Enterprise Fund

Counterpart Enterprise Fund (CEF) was set up in 1998 by Counterpart International with USAID grant funding to establish a microfinance facility in the Khabarovsh region (in the framework of the Far East Microfinance Program). The fund provides individual and group loans to entrepreneurs in retail trading and wholesale and consumer services. Individual loans (collateralized) of up to $30,000 are disbursed to small businesses and sole proprietors who have been in operation for at least six months. Group loans ranging from $1,000 to 10,000 are disbursed to groups of three to five borrowers under mutual guarantee (collateral is required for loans over $5,000). Both group and individual loans are for periods of up to 18 months. Since its establishment, CEF has extended credit to over 3,700 small businesses, with loans totaling $15 million.

Sakhalin Regional Microfinance Program

The Sakhalin Regional Microfinance Program was launched in 1999 to develop a network of sustainable MFIs providing credit to small businesses and sole proprietors in the Sakhalin region. The program is implemented by ACDI/VOCA and financed by USAID. A network of four program offices in the South of Sakhalin offer two basic credit products: peer group loans (no collateral required) and individual loans (collateralized). Peer group loans are disbursed to groups of 5–10 borrowers under mutual guarantee. Group loan size ranges from $500 to 5,000 per person. Individual loans range from $5,000 to 50,000, with a maturity of up to 24 months. As of end of February 2004, the program had disbursed about 6,000 loans totaling about $11 million, the majority of them peer group loans. In May 2003, the Sakhalin Small Business Credit Society (the entity established to run the program) secured its first $200,000 credit from a local bank (Dolinsk Bank); the loan was repaid in full on schedule. The Sakhalin Program also received a donation for additional loan capital from Exxon-Mobil and SakWest to support local entrepreneurship.

Microfinance Programs in the North Caucasus

The Danish Refugee Council (DRC) has been operating a microcredit operation in the Stavropol Krai since 1998. In 2002, DRC expanded its microcredit operation to Ingushetia and Chechnya. The program operates on a subsidized basis (no interest rates are charged on microloans). DRC is planning to establish a spin-off MFI to take over the microcredit program and make it financially sustainable over time. DRC's current outstanding credit portfolio in Ingushetia and Chechnya amounts to $300,000 with about 400 active clients. Average loan size is $870. Loans are made primarily to micro-entrepreneurs engaged in small trading and cattle raising.

On November 1, 2004, UNDP also launched a recovery program in the North Caucasus. The United Nations has been working in the region for several years to integrate refugees and forced migrants from other parts of Russia. Whereas assistance to date has primarily focused on humanitarian relief, the UNDP recovery program will aim to stimulate economic activity and facilitate micro and small business development. One of the first planned program activities aims to identify existing potential delivery channels and build up local microfinance institutions.

Russian Regional Funds Involved in the Provision of Microfinance Services (with Federal Fund Participation)

Statement on the Implementation of Microfinancing Programs by SME Support Funds
Provided by the Russian Federal Fund for Small Business Support

–	Stakeholders of program implementation	Credit portfolio (Rub, 000)	Implementation term		Allowance of microcredit				Number of borrowers
			Start	End	Rate %	Value (Rub, 000)	Term	Number Of units	
1	Tula Oblast SME support fund	14,495.00	03/09/00	07/05/04	3%	10–150	2–6 mo.	193	130
2	Fund to Support Small Business and to Foster Competition of the Republic of Adygeya	18,922.50	12/25/00 12/08/06	02/22/03 01/15/06	3%	10–100	up to 6 mo.	166	112
3	Orlovskaya Oblast SME support fund	139,458.00	12/25/00	02/20/03	2.5%	5–300	up to 1 year	1,645	780
4	Voronezh Oblast SME support fund	34,970.00	12/25/01 12/08/03	07/03/04 03/02/06	3–5%	5–90	1–6 mo.	2,289	1,134
5	Bolsheselskoye Municipal SME support fund	2,000.00	12/25/01	03/18/04	1.5–6 %	10-200	5–7 mo.	130	110
6	Republic of Sakha (Yakutiya) SME support fund	32,840.60	01/11/02	01/28/04	5%	10-200	5 mo.	640	324
7	Udmurdiya SME support fund	23,200.00	01/17/02	12/18/04	4%	3–100	1–9 mo.	370	255
8	Murmansk Oblast SME support fund	6,446.50	01/22/02	03/04/04	7.5%	20–150	10 days to 6 mo.	321	214
9	Pskov Oblast SME support fund	2,500.00	05/25/02	12/29/05	3-5%	5–100	3–6 mo.	228	86
10	Republic of Khakasiya SME support fund	10,144.00	06/03/02 12/08/03	12/29/05 12/29/05	4.8%	3–100	up to 6 mo.	339	265
11	Nizhegorodskaya Oblast SME support fund	8,210.00	11/15/02	01/17/05	2.4%	50–150	up to 6 mo.	328	222
12	Khabarovsk Krai SME support fund	21,000.00	11/12/02	12/18/04	5.6%	50–300	up to 1,5 mo.	76	33
13	Regional Fund to Facilitate Production of Goods and to Support Small Business in the Kuban Area	10,000.00	10/01/03	Implemen tation in progress	3.3%	10–300	1–12 mo.	200	84
14	Government Fund to Support Small Business of the Kaluga Oblast	11,000.00	04/10/02	Implemen tation in progress	2.6%	50–200	up to 6 mo.	144	96
15	Sverdlovsk Oblast Fund to Support Small Business	14,000.00	12/06/98	10/01/03	7.5%	5–60	up to 3 mo.	9,932	6,621
16	Ryazan Oblast Fund to Support Small Business	3,100.00	12/08/03	03/02/06	4.5%	50–100	2–5 mo.	42	42
17	Sochi Municipal Fund to Support Small Business	1,000.00	12/08/03	04/01/06	5%	50–100	up to 6 mo.	10	10
18	Ivanovo Government Fund to Support Small Business	400.00	12/08/03	12/29/05	5%	6,5–100	2–6 mo.	8	8
19	Municipal Fund to Facilitate Production of Goods and to Support Small Business, the city of Tuapse	1,000.00	12/08/03	03/02/06	1.3–4. 6%	100	3–5 mo.	9	9
20	Dmitrovskiy Municipal Fund to Support Small Business of the Moscow Oblast	400.00	12/08/03	03/02/06	2.5%	100	up to 6 mo.	4	4
21	Regional Fund to Support Small Business and Foster Competition of the Republic of Ingushetiya	1,000.00	12/22/03	01/15/06	1.6–1. 8%	100	up to 6 mo.	10	10
	Total	356,086.60						17,084	10,549

Illustrative List of World Bank-funded Microfinance Support Projects

Projects in Europe and Central Asia

Country and approval date	Project and amount (in $ million)	Type of support provided
Albania 1999	Microcredit 12.0	• Establishing and funding sustainable Rural Credit and Savings Associations • Technical assistance and funding to transform existing Village Credit Funds into Savings and Credit Associations • Funding the expansion of existing urban microcredit program • Developing Urban Microcredit foundation • Credit line for Urban Microcredit foundation
Albania 2001	Rural Poverty Alleviation 2.4	• Establishing and funding about 50 small Village Credit Funds
Albania 1995	Rural Development Project (Microfinance component $4.3 million)	• Technical assistance and credit to extend the activities of the Village Credit Fund • Technical assistance and credit to create a sustainable financial institution based on Riaffeisen-type (savings and credit) system for poor farmers
Azerbaijan 1999	Agricultural Development and Credit 30.0	• Technical assistance to create and strengthen Lending Financial Institutions in rural areas such as Credit Cooperatives and Solidarity Groups • Developing and strengthening the legal and regulatory framework
Bosnia-Herzegovina 2001	Local Initiatives (Microfinance) Project II 20.0	• Lending funds to MFIs that have demonstrated the capacity to be institutionally and financially viable over the long term, and also have capacity to increase their outreach (lending for 15-year period), with the aim to build up capital base and to assist MFI to leverage commercial funding • MFI legal and regulatory reform to enable MFIs to collect savings and expand their services • Microfinance sector capacity building support, through training and technical assistance • Developing research and impact assessment capability of local MFIs
Central Asia 2003	Regional Microfinance Strategy Seminar	• A seminar on donor coordination with the participation of donor agencies, MFIs, and government officials
Central Asia 2003	Microcredit and the Poor	• A regional study to assess the microfinance industry in the region and formulate policy recommendations
Kyrgyz Republic 1997	Rural Finance 16.0	• Developing community-based rural financial institutions and social collateral system based on group lending • Establishing a nonbank financial institution (Kyrgyz Agricultural Financial Institution, or KAFC) to provide lending to the agricultural and agribusiness sectors • Establishing Small Credit Outreach Program (SFCOP) line of credit • Technical assistance and training programs to KAFC and SFCOP
Kyrgyz Republic 1999	Rural Finance II 15.0	• Providing a credit line to KAFC and other eligible commercial banks • Technical assistance to KAFC for institutional development such as strengthening lending operations, risk management, asset and liability management, and internal audit
Romania 2001	Rural Finance 80.0	• Establishing Rural Credit and Leasing Facility, which will provide microloans and leasing to rural entrepreneurs
Tajikistan 2001	Microfinance Institutions Development Technical Assistance 44,000	• Technical assistance for institutional capacity building
Tajikistan 1999	Farm Privatization Support Project 20.0	• Establishing Rural Savings and Credit Associations
Tajikistan 2002	Poverty Alleviation Project II (1.36 Microfinance component; total project cost: 18.28)	• Establishing a credit line for MFIs
Ukraine 2004	Rural Finance Project 125.00	• Establishing Rural Credit and Leasing Facility credit line, to provide microloans and leasing to rural entrepreneurs through eligible private banks and private leasing companies • Financing banks and other intermediaries such as credit unions, leasing companies, and bonded warehouses to establish and operate a network of rural banking and microcredit offices • Upgrading legal regulatory and institutional framework for rural finance
Uzbekistan 2001	Rural Enterprise Support 36.14	• Setting up a rural finance facility through eligible financial institutions to provide small loans to private farms and rural businesses

Selected Projects from Other Regions

Country	Project	Approval date	Type of support provided
Bangladesh	Financial Services for the Poorest 5.0	2002	• Financing Revolving Loan Funds • Setting up financial services for the Poorest Unit • Training staff and borrowers • Establishing a Disaster Fund to compensate the borrowers for the losses caused by natural disasters • Designing and implementing sound monitoring and evaluation system
Brazil	Northeast Microfinance Development Project 50.0	2000	• Providing technical assistance in the form of training, equipment to support the sustainable growth of CrediAmigo
Madagascar	Microfinance Project 16.4	1999	• Creating a framework for developing savings and loan associations and other MFIs • Developing the local capacity to establish MFIs • Training and engaging government officials, NGOs, and other participants
Mongolia	Sustainable Livelihood Project 18.73	2002	• Creating a Microfinance Development Fund, which would lend to accredited MFIs • Strengthening Revolving Loan Funds • Development of index-based livestock insurance scheme

List of Microfinance Commercial Funding Sources

#	Name of investor	Country of incorporation	Year of inception	Type of investment	Eligible partners	Region of investment	Fund's assets, ($ mln)	Number of active microfinance investmts
1	Accion Gateway Fund (Accion Gateway Fund L.L.C.)	U.S.	1996	Loans and debt securities, equity investments	Bank, nonbank fin. inst.	Latin America and the Caribbean	5.0	8
2	Alterfin	Belgium	1995	Loans and debt securities, equity investments, technical assistance	Bank, NGO, credit union, cooperative, nonbank fin. inst.	Africa, East Asia and the Pacific, Latin America and the Caribbean, Middle East and North Africa	5.0	16
3	**BlueOrchard Finance**		—	—				
4	Calvert Community Investments (Calvert Foundation)	U.S.	1990	Loans and debt securities	Bank, NGO, credit union, cooperative, nonbank fin. inst.	Africa, East Asia and the Pacific, Latin America and the Caribbean, Middle East and North Africa, Eastern Europe and Central Asia, North America, South Asia	8.5	32
5	Citigroup Foundation	U.S.	1980	Loans and debt securities, grants, guarantees, technical assistance	Nonprofit (NGO)	Africa, East Asia and the Pacific, Latin America and the Caribbean, Middle East and North Africa, Eastern Europe and Central Asia, North America, South Asia, Western Europe	63.0	42
6	CORDAID (Catholic Organisation for Relief and Development AID)	Netherlands	1997	Loans and debt securities, grants, guarantees, technical assistance, equity investments	Bank, NGO, credit union, cooperative, nonbank fin. inst.	Latin America and the Caribbean, Africa, Middle East and North Africa, East Asia and the Pacific	20.0	75
7	Deutsche Bank Microcredit Development Fund	U.S.	1997	Loans and debt securities	Bank, NGOs, credit union, cooperative, nonbank fin. inst.	Africa, East Asia and the Pacific, Latin America and the Caribbean, Middle East and North Africa, Eastern Europe and Central Asia, North America, South Asia, Western Europe	2.3	20
8	Deutsche Investitions- und Entwicklungsgesellschaft GmbH	Germany	1999	Loans and debt securities, guarantees, equity investments	Bank, nonbank fin. inst., start-up specialized microfinance bank, investment fund wholesale intermediaries	Africa, East Asia and the Pacific, Eastern Europe and Central Asia, Latin America and the Caribbean	1,550	6
9	Dexia Microcredit Fund	Luxembourg	1998	Loans and debt securities, guarantees	Bank, nonbank financial institution, rural bank, NGO, credit union, cooperative	World	22.5	29
10	Fonds International de Garantie	Switzerland	1996	Guarantees	Bank, nonbank financial institution, NGO, credit union, cooperative	Latin America and the Caribbean, Africa	2.06	20
11	Geisse Foundation	U.S.	1996	Loans and debt securities, equity investments, technical assistance, grants, guarantees	Bank, nonbank financial institution, nonprofit (NGO)	East Asia and the Pacific, Latin America and the Caribbean	n.a.	1
12	The Hivos-Triodos Fund	Netherlands	1994	Loans and debt securities, equity investments, guarantees	Bank, nonbank financial institution, NGO, credit union, cooperatives	Eastern Europe and Central Asia, Latin America and the Caribbean, Africa, South Asia	9.5	26
13	Idyll Development Foundation	U.S.	1992	Loans and debt securities, equity investments	Bank, nonbank financial institution, rural bank, NGO, credit union, cooperatives	East Asia and the Pacific, Latin America and the Caribbean, North America, South Asia	2	28
14	IMI (Internationale Micro Investitionen Aktiengesellschaft)	Germany	1999	Equity investments	Bank, nonbank fin. inst.	Africa, East Asia and the Pacific, Eastern Europe and Central Asia, Latin America and the Caribbean	15.65	17

#	Name of investor	Country of incorporation	Year of inception	Type of investment	Eligible partners	Region of Investment	Fund's assets, ($ mln)	Number of active microfinance investments
15	Khula Enterprise Finance Limited	South Africa	1996	Loans and debt security, equity investments, grants, guarantees, technical assistance	—	Africa	n.a.	n.a.
16	Kreditanstalt für Wiederaufbau	Germany	1948	Loans and debt security, grants, guarantees	Bank, nonbank fin. inst., NGO, start-up specialized microfinance bank, private and state-owned bank	Eastern Europe and Central Asia	85.4	31
17	Kolibri Kapital ASA	Norway	2000	Loans and debt security	Nonbank fin. inst., cooperative, credit union, NGO	Latin America and the Caribbean	n.a.	1
18	Latin American Bridge Fund	U.S.	1984	Guarantees	Bank, nonbank fin. inst., NGO	Latin America and the Caribbean	7.2	6
19	La Fayette Participations, Horus Banque et Finance	France	2001	Equity investments, technical assistance	Bank, nonbank fin. inst., cooperative, credit union	Africa, East Asia and the Pacific, Eastern Europe and Central Asia, Middle East and Africa, South Asia	0.2	3
20	Luxmint - ADA	Luxembourg	1994	Loans and debt security, equity investments, guarantees, technical assistance	Bank, nonbank fin. inst., cooperative, credit union, NGO	Africa, Latin America and the Caribbean	1,193,150	11
21	Microfinance Alliance Fund	Philippines	2000	Loans and debt security, technical assistance	Bank, nonbank fin. inst., cooperative, credit union, NGO	East Asia and the Pacific	1.7	10
22	Multilateral Investment Fund	U.S.	1993	Loans and debt securities, equity investments, technical assistance, grants, guarantees	—	Latin America and the Caribbean	n.a.	13
23	NOVIB	Netherlands	1996	—	Bank, nonbank fin. inst., cooperative, credit union, NGO	Africa, East Asia and the Pacific, Eastern Europe and Central Asia, Latin America and the Caribbean, South Asia	n.a.	34
24	Oikocredit	Netherlands	1975	Loans and debt securities, equity investments, technical assistance, guarantees	Bank, nonbank fin. inst., cooperative, credit union, NGO	Africa, East Asia and the Pacific, Eastern Europe and Central Asia, Latin America and the Caribbean, South Asia	155.0	75
25	Partnership Fund and FONIDI Fund	Canada	1996	Loans and debt securities, equity investments, guarantees	Bank, nonbank financial institution, rural bank, NGO, credit union, cooperative	Africa, Latin America and the Caribbean	10.0	2
26	PlaNet Finance - Revolving Credit Fund	France	2000	Loans and debt security	Nonbank financial institution, rural bank, NGO, credit union, cooperative	—	0.2	7
27	ProFund International	Panama	1995	Loans and debt securities, equity investments	Bank, nonbank financial institution	Latin America and the Caribbean	22.6	11
28	Sarona Global Investment Fund	U.S.	2000	Loans and debt securities, equity investments	Bank, nonbank financial institution	Latin America and the Caribbean	4.5	3
29	Societe d'Investissement et de Developpement International	France	1983	Loans and debt securities, equity investments, technical assistance	Bank, nonbank financial institution, rural bank, NGO, credit union, cooperative	Africa, East Asia and the Pacific, Latin America and the Caribbean, Middle East and North Africa, Eastern Europe and Central Asia, North America, South Asia	2.8	27
30	Triodos-Doen Foundation	Netherlands	1994	Loans and debt securities, equity investments, guarantees	Bank, nonbank financial institution, NGO, credit union, cooperative	Africa, East Asia and the Pacific, Latin America and the Caribbean, Middle East and North Africa, Eastern Europe and Central Asia, South Asia	21.5	24
31	Unitus	U.S.	2000	Loans and debt securities, equity investments, technical assistance, grants, guarantees	Bank, nonbank financial institution, rural bank, NGO	Africa, East Asia and the Pacific, Latin America and the Caribbean, Middle East and North Africa, South Asia	1.9	1

—. Not available.

Source: "Central Asia Microfinance and the Poor," ECSSD, World Bank, 2003.

CBR Statutory Requirements (Instruction No. 62A)

B anks argue that CBR Instruction No. 62A of June 30, 1997 on the Procedure for the Establishment and Usage of the Provision for Probable Credit Losses (hereinafter "PPCL Instruction")[55] currently acts as a "loan bottleneck" limiting the banks' willingness and ability to originate small loans. The strict and highly formalized categories of risks and associated provisioning requirements for credits under this instruction can make the extension of a loan, especially to SMEs with a less than exemplary or no previous credit history and loan performance, a cumbersome and costly procedure for banks. This argument is detailed below:

- The provision for probable losses has to be established separately for every credit extended.[56] This approach does not allow banks to take a pooling approach when evaluating risks and allocating reserves and may act as a disincentive to bankers who would extend loans as long as they could take advantage of the economies of scale provided by a portfolio approach to credit risk management and lending operations.
- A loan "remade" for example under a renewal agreement, shall per se be categorized as a "bad debt."[57] Similarly, in case of the borrower's repaying the credit or interest on account of a new credit given to the borrower by the same or a connected bank, such new credit is per se to be classified as "bad credit."[58] These classifications,

---

55. In the wording of Direction of the Central Bank of the Russian Federation No. 101-U of December 25, 1997 (with the Amendments and Addenda of May 12, July 24, December 28, 1998; March 5, July 13, August 2, 1999; May 24, 2000; and March 1, 2001). Translation used: http://site.securities.com/cgi-bin/add_layout/94dec/Data/RU/Garant/Docs/12008460.html#200.
56. PPCL Instruction, Sec. 3.6.
57. PPCL Instruction, Sec. 2.8.4.
58. PPCL Instruction, Sec. 2.13.

respectively, can (1) have a direct impact on performance ratios and on earnings (since bad debts must be 100 percent reserved) and (2) discourage banks from working with troubled borrowers and remaking loans or refinancing loans.

■ When a single borrower has obtained credits under several credit agreements, for purposes of establishing the provision, all of the borrower's debts are to be attributed to the group of maximum risk assigned under one of the given credits. A reclassification may only take place when the borrower has repaid the credit earlier attributed to the maximum risk group.[59] This approach may act as a disincentive to banks, which consider lending to enterprises with less than exemplary credit histories and loan performance, because they would continually be forced to tie up earnings in reserve accounts.

■ If one borrower has obtained a credit classified in risk group 2, 3, or 4 ("non-standard," "doubtful," or "bad," respectively), every further credit extended to this borrower is to be attributed to the same group of credit risk.[60] This approach does not allow lending banks to recognize a higher degree of loan protection through strong collateral. Moreover, bankers will be hesitant to extend a new credit when the consequence will be a higher percentage of loans in risk categories 2, 3, and 4, as well as a higher amount of unpaid principal and interest subject to adverse classification, since ratios of classified loans and classified loan balances are often used as quantitative measures of a bank's health.

■ On a more general note, given CBR's emphasis on the borrower's demonstrated ability to repay and the level of credit security (reflected in various provisions under the PPCL Instruction), banks are reluctant to consider other aspects—such as unreported incomes or savings, reputation, or business outlook—when underwriting loans. Similarly, the required amounts of provision are strictly set and attributed to the risk groups, not leaving any range for banks within which they could exercise their judgment when allocating reserves.

---

59. PPCL Instruction, Sec. 2.10.
60. PPCL Instruction, Sec. 2.9.

Regional Comparative
Benchmark Tables

INSTITUTIONAL CHARACTERISTICS	Definition	All MFIs	Africa	Asia	ECA	LAC	MENA
Number of MFIs	Sample size of group	231	57	57	49	52	16
Age	Years functioning as an MFI	9	7	12	5	13	7
Total assets	Total assets, adjusted for inflation and standardized loan portfolio provisioning and write-offs	32,410,823	9,113,640	81,198,092	10,719,008	31,863,457	9,812,513
Offices	Number, including head office	48	23	138	12	18	29
Personnel	Total number of employees	376	149	1,039	83	236	170

FINANCIAL STRUCTURE	Definition	All MFIs	Africa	Asia	ECA	LAC	MENA
Capital/asset ratio	Total equity, adjusted/total assets, adjusted	44.1%	41.8%	31.5%	64.0%	32.2%	74.7%
Commercial funding liabilities ratio	All liabilities with "market" price/ gross loan portfolio	63.2%	103.7%	72.4%	21.8%	61.8%	17.6%
Debt/equity ratio	Total liabilities, adjusted/total equity , adjusted	2.2	–3.2	5.0	1.3	6.4	.5
Deposits to loans	Voluntary savings/gross loan portfolio, adjusted	43.0%	91.9%	51.4%	7.4%	26.9%	0.0%
Deposits to total assets	Voluntary savings/total assets, adjusted	19.6%	27.1%	29.2%	5.2%	20.6%	0.0%
Gross loan portfolio/ total assets	Gross loan portfolio, adjusted/total assets, adjusted	70.5%	59.2%	69.8%	79.6%	76.0%	67.4%

SCALE AND OUTREACH	Definition	All MFIs	Africa	Asia	ECA	LAC	MENA
Number of active borrowers	Number of borrowers with loans outstanding	47,688	26,285	130,169	5,840	31,424	25,561
Percentage of women borrowers	Number of active women borrowers/ number of active borrowers	60.2%	62.5%	64.2%	65.6%	38.1%	78.2%
Gross loan portfolio	Gross loan portfolio, adjusted for standardized write-offs	19,214,376	5,800,360	40,132,314	8,510,944	25,176,261	5,884,795
Average loan balance per borrower	Gross loan portfolio/number of active borrowers	689	370	402	1,263	903	348
Average loan balance per borrower/gross national income per capita	Average loan balance per borrower/ gross national income per capita	74.7%	124.6%	53.9%	73.0%	59.9%	19.9%
Number of voluntary savers	Number of savers with passbook and time deposit accounts	27,621	31,100	61,134	763	17,381	0
Voluntary savings	Total value of passbook and time deposit accounts	19,270,139	3,680,225	58,680,859	2,626,406	14,771,660	0
Average savings balance per saver	Voluntary savings/number of voluntary savers	841	1,411	169	2,842	618	0

PROFITABILITY AND SUSTAINABILITY	Definition	All MFIs	Africa	Asia	ECA	LAC	MENA
Adjusted return on assets	Net operating income, adjusted and net of taxes/average total assets	-0.8%	–4.6%	1.2%	-0.3%	-0.2%	2.1%
Adjusted return on equity	Net operating income, adjusted and net of taxes/average total equity	5.9%	–4.6%	12.4%	1.2%	15.6%	2.8%
Operational self-sufficiency	Financial revenue/(financial expense + net loan loss provision expense + operating expense)	122.8%	117.1%	128.0%	130.7%	117.3%	118.3%
Financial self-sufficiency	Financial revenue, adjusted/ (financial expense + net loan loss provision expense + operating expense), adjusted	107.7%	94.4%	118.8%	109.3%	108.8%	106.5%

REVENUE	Definition	All MFIs	Africa	Asia	ECA	LAC	MENA
Adjusted financial revenue ratio	Financial revenue, adjusted/ average total assets	29.1%	26.4%	26.5%	33.5%	31.4%	26.9%
Adjusted profit margin	Net operating income, adjusted/ financial revenue, adjusted	–15.7%	–34.1%	–7.7	–3.7%	–16.7%	–11.9%

Yield on gross portfolio (nominal)	Financial revenue from loan portfolio/average gross loan portfolio	38.7%	40.1%	35.2%	42.4%	37.5%	39.1%
Yield on gross portfolio (real)	(Yield on gross portfolio (nominal) - inflation rate)/(1 + inflation rate)	29.5%	23.3%	31.3%	33.9%	28.1%	35.3%
EXPENSE	**Definition**	**All MFIs**	**Africa**	**Asia**	**ECA**	**LAC**	**MENA**
Adjusted total expense ratio	(Financial expense + net loan loss provision expense + operating expense), adjusted/average total assets	29.4%	30.7%	25.0%	32.9%	31.0%	24.8%
Adjusted financial expense ratio	Financial expense, adjusted/ average total assets	7.1%	7.6%	6.3%	6.9%	8.9%	2.9%
Adjusted loan loss provision expense ratio	Net loan loss provision expense, adjusted/average total assets	2.3%	2.3%	2.9%	1.5%	3.3%	-0.2%
Adjusted operating expense ratio	Operating expense, adjusted/ average total assets	20.0%	20.7%	15.9%	24.6%	18.9%	22.1%
Adjusted personnel expense ratio	Personnel expense, adjusted/ average total assets	11.0%	10.4%	9.1%	13.3%	10.5%	13.8%
Adjusted administrative expense ratio	Administrative expense, adjusted/ average total assets	9.1%	10.2%	6.8%	11.3%	8.4%	8.3%
Adjustment expense ratio	Net inflation and subsidized cost-of-funds adjustment expense/average total assets	3.8%	5.8%	2.0%	4.5%	3.5%	2.2%
EFFICIENCY	**Definition**	**All MFIs**	**Africa**	**Asia**	**ECA**	**LAC**	**MENA**
Operating expense/ loan portfolio	Operating expense, adjusted/ average gross loan portfolio	33.2%	43.8%	26.0%	33.7%	26.8%	39.9%
Personnel expense/ loan portfolio	Personnel expense, adjusted/ average gross loan portfolio	17.9%	21.3%	15.0%	17.9%	14.7%	26.2%
Average salary/gross national income per capita	Average personnel expense, adjusted/gross national income per capita	748.4%	1,341.9%	422.2%	670.9%	629.3%	420.9%
Adjusted cost per borrower	Operating expense, adjusted/ average number of active borrowers	158	129	50	299	181	121
PRODUCTIVITY	**Definition**	**All MFIs**	**Africa**	**Asia**	**ECA**	**LAC**	**MENA**
Borrowers per staff member	Number of active borrowers/number of personnel	136	164	144	84	146	138
Borrowers per loan officer	Number of active borrowers/number of loan officers	269	334	274	151	323	210
Voluntary savers per staff member	Number of voluntary savers/number of personnel	110	166	171	7	120	0
Personnel allocation ratio	Number of loan officers/number of personnel	53.7%	53.9%	55.1%	56.0%	45.7%	67.8%
PORTFOLIO QUALITY	**Definition**	**All MFIs**	**Africa**	**Asia**	**ECA**	**LAC**	**MENA**
Portfolio at risk > 30 days	Outstanding balance, loans overdue> 30 days/gross loan portfolio, adjusted	5.2%	7.5%	7.0%	2.1%	4.3%	2.2%
Portfolio at risk > 90 days	Outstanding balance, loans overdue> 90 days/gross loan portfolio, adjusted	2.8%	3.9%	3.8%	1.1%	2.5%	1.5%
Write-off ratio	Value of loans written off/adjusted average gross loan portfolio	3.0%	3.0%	3.1%	1.6%	4.2%	2.6%
Loan loss rate	Adjusted write-offs, net of recoveries/adjusted average gross loan portfolio	2.5%	2.9%	2.9%	1.3%	4.0%	-0.5%
Risk coverage	Loan loss reserve, adjusted/PAR > 30 days	278.7%	192.7%	261.6%	372.2%	281.6%	368.3%

Note: Eastern Europe and Central Asia (ECA); Latin America and the Caribbean (LAC); Middle-East and North Africa (MENA). For further information regarding the adjustments and statistical issues used in this report, log on to http://www.mixmbb.org.
Source: Mix Bulletin, May 2005.

References

Buyske, Gail. 2005. "Financing Russia's Real Entrepreneurs." Unpublished manuscript, January.

CGAP. 2002. CGAP Donor Brief No.2, April.

———. 2004. CGAP Occasional Paper No.8, July.

Cordonnier, Christopher. 2004. *Development of a National System of Rural Cooperative Banking in Russia: Some Proposals Based on International Experience.* UNDP's Russian Farm Entrepreneurs Development Program.

EBRD. 2003. Project Evaluation Department Special Study of RSBF, July.

Foster, Sarah, Seth Greene, and Justina Pytkowska. June 2003. *The State of Microfinance in Central and Eastern Europe and the New Independent States.*

MIX. 2005. "Benchmarking Microfinance in Eastern Europe and Central Asia."

Nowak, Maria. 2005. *On ne prete (PAS) qu'aux riches.*

Perttunen, Paula. 2004. Keynote speech, Investment Conference, Helsinki, October.

Rajan, Raghuram G., and Luigi Zingales. *Saving Capitalism from the Capitalists.*

SME Resource Center. 2003. "Analysis of Microfinance Development in Russia." Moscow.

TACIS. 2001. Microfinance study.

World Bank. 2001. *World Bank Development Report 2000–2001.*

———. 2003. Report on Central Asia. June.

———. 2004a. "Brazil—Access to Financial Services," World Bank Report No. 27773-BR, February 2004.

———. 2004b. Proceedings of World Bank Workshop on Cooperative Financial Institutions and Access to Finance, March.

———. 2004c. "Russian Federation—Poverty Assessment."

———. 2004d. World Bank Quarterly Economic Review. World Bank Moscow Office.

World Bank and Open Society Institute. 2003. *The Microfinance Revolution: Sustainable Finance for the Poor.* Volume 1.

Eco-Audit

Environmental Benefits Statement

The World Bank is committed to preserving Endangered Forests and natural resources. We print World Bank Working Papers and Country Studies on 100 percent postconsumer recycled paper, processed chlorine free. The World Bank has formally agreed to follow the recommended standards for paper usage set by Green Press Initiative—a nonprofit program supporting publishers in using fiber that is not sourced from Endangered Forests. For more information, visit www.greenpressinitiative.org.

In 2004, the printing of these books on recycled paper saved the following:

Trees*	Solid Waste	Water	Net Greenhouse Gases	Electricity
307	14,387	130,496	28,262	52,480
'40" in height and 6-8" in diameter	Pounds	Gallons	Pounds	KWH